Challenge English

조동인 저

도서출판 **진 영 사**

Challenge English

조동인 저

2017년 12월 18일 초판 인쇄
2017년 12월 20일 초판 발행
2020년 03월 11일 초판2쇄 발행

발행인 박 진 영
발행처 도서출판 진영사
인천광역시 부평구 갈산동 185번지 풍진빌딩 303호
전화 : 032)505-4207
팩스 : 032)505-4206
E-mail : 0183734207@hanmail.net
등록 : 122-91-77317

ISBN 978-89-6541-340-0 93740
값 14,000원

머 리 말

영어가 국제화시대에 의사소통을 위한 필수 요소라는 것은 이제는 두말하면 잔소리가 되었다. 대학 졸업생들의 취업이 갈수록 치열해지는 한국의 취업 시장에서 영어를 잘하는 것은 더 이상 장점이 아닌 것으로 여겨지기까지 한다. 하지만, 영어를 어느 정도 하는 사람은 많아도 영어를 잘하는 사람은 아직도 많지 않은 것이 현실이다. 이번에 집필한 English Challenge는 다양한 상황에서의 회화 구사능력을 향상시키고 영어를 잘하기 위한 필수적인 학습 요소를 담았다. 현실에서 일어날 수 있는 상황을 설정하고 회화구사 능력을 향상시키는 것에 초점을 맞추었고 이를 위해 다양한 Challenge를 수행할 수 있도록 구성하였다. 영어는 조금씩이라도 매일 매일 공부하고 연습하는 것이 중요하다. 영어에 애로를 겪는 학생들이 이 교재를 통해 영어 회화실력 향상에 많은 도움을 받고 유창한 영어를 구사하는 실력자가 되길 저자로서 간절히 기원하는 바이다.

2017년 11월 20일

저자 올림

Contents

Chapter 1 Teaching

Dialogue Challenge 1

Karl : You teach the students of a middle school English.

Janet : Yes, I do.

Karl : How many years of teaching experience do you have?

Janet : About 10 years.

Karl : Wow, you must be an excellent teacher.

Janet : I hope so, but as you know, to learn is one thing, and to teach is another.

Karl : Definitely you are right.

Janet : Are you happy when you teach the students English?

Karl : At the beginning stage of my career, teaching is my dream job, but now I lost much interest in it.

Janet : Why did you lose your interest?

Karl : Well, I don't know, I want to know the reason.

Janet : When you teach the students English what is your difficulty?

Karl : When students don't react actively during the class I feel embarrassed.

Janet : Do you mean by that you are embarrassed when students do not pay attention to your teaching?

Karl : Yes, sort of.

Janet : Don't worry. If I were in your shoes, I would accept students behavior innocently. And I would not make any prejudice on them. Try to open the minds of students naturally. When they open their minds they put much focus on the classes. Additionally You are a born teacher. You have a great talent in teaching students. I know you will do a good job.

Karl : Thank you for your advice.

Janet : You are a great teacher as far as I know. You are doing well so far.

Karl : In fact, I am worried that I should change my job and career. But your tips give me much energy.

Janet : Never worry. You are a wonderful teacher. Keep up the good work.

Karl : Thank you. Actually I am happy when students ask me questions during the class. I will do much efforts to make better classes for the students.

Janet : Very nice! You are going in the right direction.

Sentence Challenge 1

01. How many years of teaching experience do you have?

02. To learn is one thing, and to teach is another.

03. Why did you lose your interest?

04. When you teach the students English what is your difficulty?

05. When students don't react actively during the class I feel embarrassed.

06. Do you mean by that you are embarrassed when students do not pay attention to your teaching?

07. If I were in your shoes, I would accept students behavior innocently.

08. I would not make any prejudice on them.

09. Your tips give me much energy.

10. Keep up the good work.

11. I will do much efforts to make better classes for the students.

12. You are going in the right direction.

Grammar Challenge 1

How + often do you~~

It is quite a good and easy pattern you can use. After the word, "how" you add up any kinds of adjective. In this page, "often is applied". It is a very useful expression for the conversation between people.

The examples are as follows:

"How often do you give your parents call?"
"How often do you go to the movies?"
"How often do you help your parents?"
"How often do you study English?"
"How often do you go to church a year?"
"How often do you clean up your house?"
"How often do you meet your boy friend?"
"How often do you exercise a month?"
"How often do you talk to your friends a day?"
"How often do you drink water a day?"
"How often do you eat pizza a month?"

Paragraph Challenge 1

Questions 1–4 refer to the following paragraph.

Ten years ago, Mrs. Kimberly signed a three-year rent to open her fancy restaurant, Kimberly Cuisine, at Kensington Avenue. Mrs. Kimberly were happy with many 1._______ these days. "Our dishes are based on fresh and organic ingredients" she was very proud of the fact. But actually Mrs. Kimberly 2. _______ from the low profit at the beginning stage. Nowadays, the restaurant is very 3._______ and became a famous place in the region. Additionally she is planning to open 4._______ branch at Plum Avenue.

01. (A) person
(B) porters
(C) customers
(D) waiters

02. (A) suffered
(B) frustrated
(C) pleased
(D) booked

03. (A) crowd
(B) crowded
(C) crowds
(D) crowding

04. (A) other
(B) another
(C) others
(D) anothers

Conversation Challenge 1

01. Where's your company located?

(A) On Pine Street

(B) No, it wasn't expensive.

(C) Location is convenient.

02. When is the end of the today's conference?

(A) At the News stand

(B) Conference is important.

(C) Around 12 o'clock

03. Where is the annual ceremony held?

(A) Yes, it was across here.

(B) I know it is true.

(C) At the auditorium.

04. **Who's the CEO of your company next year?**

(A) In this town

(B) The stage

(C) Mrs. Watson

05. **Where do you think the orientation for the new comers will be held?**

(A) Starting next year

(B) In this conference room

(C) For the comers

06. **Have you ever met with your new client?**

(A) Yes, I already met her.

(B) No, they didn't.

(C) That's a new project.

07. **Are you going to go to the movies this weekend?**

(A) I've gone to the movies.

(B) A new seasonal movie

(C) Sure, I and Jennifer will go there.

08. **Is the department store near here?**

(A) It stores 100 giga bites.

(B) It's an expensive department store.

(C) Yes, it is 1 mile away.

09. **Where should I put the parcel, ma'am?**

(A) Right over there.

(B) By next morning

(C) Mr. Parkerson will take care of the parcel.

10. **Can you please show me how to turn on the air conditioner?**

(A) Yes, I can help you.

(B) It's already ten o'clock.

(C) Please show me the way.

11. **Would you give me a hand to make some copies of the report?**

(A) Yes, I can. anytime call me.

(B) It makes good copies.

(C) Yes, for ten years.

12. **Where did you get the management consulting?**

(A) I'll have nowhere.

(B) From the Mckinge Company.

(C) Two hours of consulting

13. **Who is the new applicant for the company?**

(A) I think Mrs. Pamela.

(B) Several applicants

(C) I plan to give the new resume.

14. **How many times a day do the express trains stop here?**

(A) 10 dollars

(B) Turn to the left.

(C) At least 25.

15. **How can I find the way to fix may broken notebook computer?**

(A) You'd better consult the repair and maintenance department.

(B) That's what I am saying.

(C) Try the computer.

16. **Shall we buy more papers for the printer?**

(A) No, they're enough now.

(B) Yes, we're quite busy.

(C) Papers are expensive.

17. **The company is going to be out of business at the end of the year.**

(A) Yes, I am sorry to hear that.

(B) The business is not ready yet.

(C) Do you know the company's CEO?

18. **When does the performance of the idol group begin?**

(A) At around 7:00 p.m.

(B) He performs well.

(C) The group is large.

19. **I'd like to have a newly ordered refrigerator in the kitchen.**

(A) She is in the kitchen.

(B) You can have new one this afternoon.

(C) A collection of refrigerators

20. **We should change the date of our board meeting next week.**

(A) The board of directors will not come today.

(B) Okay, when do you want?

(C) About 100 people at the meeting

21. **Why was the annual ceremony postponed?**

(A) I'll postpone the ceremony.

(B) The CEO is in the hospital.

(C) The ceremony is enormous.

22. **How can I get to the museum of the arts?**

(A) You'd better take a taxi. It is quite a far way.

(B) Sure, I'll go to the museum.

(C) Only for 20 days.

23. **We should finish this project by tomorrow.**

(A) Don't worry. Let me help you.

(B) On Pine Street.

(C) Let's find another project.

24. **Was Mr. Karlbertson at the seminar yesterday?**

(A) It was informative.

(B) Yes, he attended there.

(C) From the seminary

25. **Is it cheaper to buy the TV set on the internet?**

(A) Two million dollars

(B) It is quite a good quality.

(C) Much lower than the stores

26. **Why wasn't Mr. Parker able to attend the meeting?**

(A) From the meeting.

(B) He is out of town for his business trip.

(C) Sometime next week.

27. **Can't you find the way to boost the sales of the goods?**

(A) I think the goods have good quality.

(B) I did, but the market is very hostile.

(C) We all had good sales.

28. **How many people are working on the new subsidiary?**

(A) About 300

(B) There's a new company.

(C) We work hard.

29. **Can I have a feed on this new project.**

(A) Feed a new cat.

(B) Please check your email, I already sent it.

(C) Let's have a new project.

30. **Who will help to move the boxes on the desk of Mr. Karlson?**

(A) Don't worry. we already did the job.

(B) He is not ready.

(C) A couple of hours ago.

Chapter 2 How about the company?

Dialogue Challenge 2

Karl : Janet, I know you are employed by General Motors. How about the company?

Janet : Actually, I am still working for a production line that makes compact cars.
And first of all, it was a good job for me because I worked from 2 o'clock in the afternoon until 8 in the evening. I could have a good time, since I don't have to get up early in the morning. It is painful for me to get up early in the morning.

Karl : Quite intriguing. Can I join your company if there are any openings?

Janet : It depends on the condition of the company's human resources. I believe we need more personnel, since we are working overnight to meet the demand of new cars which were launched last month.

Karl : How did you get a job from General Motors? Did you have a chance to have a job interview or something?

Janet : Actually, I tried to write an impressive resume, I thought the strategy to write a detailed and informative resume was effective.

Karl : Wow! That's great. I should keep the strategy in mind.

Janet : Believe it or not, heaven helps those who help themselves.

Karl : You are right. I am trying to be a diligent person to seek a reasonable job for me. But that's not easy at all.

Karl : How about the payment satisfaction? Are you satisfied with the payroll and fringe benefits from your company?

Janet : You will know that beggars can't be choosers. It is my joke.

Honestly, I am not contented with the present pay system, but it is really hard to find out another job due to the deteriorating job market in the country.

Karl : Do you have any intent to move to another company?

Janet : Absolutely, On account of the chance I am hesitating to sign a contract with the present company next month.

Karl : Wow. I really envy you. I hope I can get a job from even a small company before the graduation of the school.

Janet : Don't worry. There is an old proverb. Every dog has his day.

Sentence Challenge 2

01. I know you are employed by General Motors.

02. I am still working for a production line that makes compact cars.

03. It is painful for me to get up early in the morning.

04. Can I join your company if there are any openings?

05. It depends on the condition of the company's human resources.

06. We are working overnight to meet the demand of new cars which were launched last month.

07. How did you get a job from General Motors?

08. Did you have a chance to have a job interview or something?

09. I tried to write an impressive resume.

10. I thought the strategy to write a detailed and informative resume was effective.

11. That's great. I should keep the strategy in mind.

12. Believe it or not, heaven helps those who help themselves.

13. Are you satisfied with the payroll and fringe benefits from your company?

14. You will know that beggars can't be choosers.

15. I am not contented with the present pay system.

16. On account of the chance I am hesitating to sign a contract with the present company next month.

17. Every dog has his day.

Grammar Challenge 2

What do you think about (verb-ing)

This question asks the opinions of people concerning some topics.

Here are some examples:

"What do you think about having a cup of coffee?"
"What do you think about applying for the company?"
"What do you think about turning on the heater?"
"What do you think about purchasing the bag?"
"What do you think about moving to another company?"
"What do you think about giving me the second chance?"
"What do you think about learning how to swim?"
"What do you think about going out with me?"
"What do you think about traveling Europe?"
"What do you think about studying hard for your future?"

Paragraph Challenge 2

Questions 1–4 refer to the following paragraph.

Thank you for your purchase of the Bright Washer. Many people are making an excellent 1.________. With a little amount of the Bright Washer, you can wash a lot of clothing clean and effectively at a time. You can have a 2.______ to save your precious money when you purchase the Bright Washer by bundles. The cleanness of the dirty clothes was already proved after 3.________ washed by the Bright Washer. So, don't 4._____ the chance of purchasing the Bright Washer. It is on sale now!

01. (A) chose
(B) choosing
(C) choosers
(D) choice

02. (A) chance
(B) challenge
(C) change
(D) check

03. (A) being
(B) proof
(C) was
(D) problem

04. (A) loose
(B) lose
(C) lost
(D) loosen

Conversation Challenge 2

01. **How would you like your coffee, Mr. Smith?**

(A) Yes, I'd like to know more.

(B) I don't know how.

(C) Cream and sugar please.

02. **Have you heard the news from CNN this morning?**

(A) No, it's old.

(B) You mean about Jason Parker?

(C) I heard about that.

03. **How about going out for lunch the weather outside is beautiful?**

(A) Yes, it sounds good.

(B) Yes, but I'll have to meet you there.

(C) No, thank you. I'm suffering from a diarrhea.

04. **Josh, do you know when our next payment is due?**

(A) It should be here any minute now.

(B) As far as I know, 10th of every month.

(C) I'll pay for it this time.

05. **Wow, you look handsome where did you get your haircut?**

(A) From the Marshall Salon.

(B) Yes, I did. Do you like it?

(C) I'm sorry. We don't like hairy products.

06. **I am sorry to ask you would like to call me back after school?**

(A) Yes, but your school picture is great.

(B) Sure, I will reach you later.

(C) In about 20 minutes, but first I'll have to change the film.

07. **Where do I speak to about getting a new cartridge?**

(A) Complete a capital equipment request form and submit it to Purchasing.

(B) I haven't asked the woman yet.

(C) I think they're using their cars.

08. **Is that man in the lobby your customer, Johnson?**

(A) Yes, he is very important person for our company.
(B) No, I've never been there before.
(C) No, but there is a similarity

09. **When are you going to take a vacation, Karl?**

(A) Yes, but I won't take it until next spring.
(B) Oh, really? When will you get back?
(C) Next month, maybe

10. **Can you finish up by the end of the month, Mr. Tellerson?**

(A) Yes, that should give me plenty of time.
(B) I was planning to do some shopping this weekend.
(C) Yes, I believe I can.

11. **Do you know that today is 30th anniversary of our company?**

(A) No, I guess I should get him a card or something.
(B) Yeah, I heard it last night.
(C) I'm not sure. I think he said it was in September.

12. **Can you tell me what time the movie, Beauty and the Beast play?**

(A) It's set in the tenth.

(B) It's only about 10 hours from here.

(C) A quarter to ten, I believe.

13. **Do we need to purchase more petroleum for the heater?**

(A) No, we have enough for another month.

(B) Yes, we'd better be prepared for the cold winter.

(C) Yes, I'd like a little more, please.

14. **How far is the Incheon train station from here?**

(A) It's only two blocks down, go past the Union bank.

(B) It doesn't stop now.

(C) We need more training sessions for the employees.

15. **How was your first blind date with a lady?**

(A) About an hour.

(B) I am feeling quite well with her.

(C) No, I don't think we have. It's nice to meet you.

16. **Is it still snowing outside, David?**

(A) No, I've finished.

(B) Yes, be careful with falling on the icy streets.

(C) No, I think it stopped.

17. **Can I help your googling, boss?**

(A) No, thank you. I can handle it.

(B) You should turn it in to the lost and found.

(C) No, thanks. I'm just browsing

18. **Would you sign up this contract with Marker and Spencer, please?**

(A) Where do I sign? Here?

(B) Yes, I think that's a good sign.

(C) No, I wouldn't. I should check more conditions.

19. **How's the new employee's work performance?**

(A) I try to get as much exercise as I can.

(B) She sings well on the stage.

(C) Actually, he is a great asset for us.

20. **Who's handling the new project, Mrs. Culberson?**

(A) Because of the holiday, we'll get paid a day early.

(B) The round ones do much better.

(C) Amie Jackson in the accounting department.

21. **Would you get me some more papers while you going out now?**

(A) I'll leave in about ten minutes.

(B) Sure, how much do you need?

(C) I'll probably take my car.

22. **Mr. President, what should I tell Mr. Johnson when he calls?**

(A) Oh, really? What did he say?

(B) Yes, you should.

(C) Tell him I am out of the town.

23. **Would you please turn off your smart phone? We are at the concert.**

(A) Sure, what do you want to hear?

(B) Yes, I like this too.

(C) Oh, I'm sorry. I will do it right now.

24. **When you are free, could you check this document, Mrs. Peggy?**

(A) No, there was nothing for you.
(B) I think it'll be here any minute.
(C) Sure, just give me two hours, sir.

25. **When are you going to have your day off?**

(A) This Friday when it is possible.
(B) Yes, but I'll probably do some work at home anyway.
(C) I did, but I took some medicine that cleared it up.

26. **How would you like your steak, sir?**

(A) That's a good price. I'll take the steak.
(B) Well done, please.
(C) Yes, I'll pay for it.

27. **Is the accountant working right with those figures?**

(A) Yes, he is doing well, don't worry.
(B) When I last saw them they were on the left.
(C) O.K, I'll take what's left.

28. **Do you want your lunch packed?**

(A) I'd like it to go, please.

(B) No, I am going to eat here.

(C) Sure, that's no problem.

29. **Are you promising to give me a pay raise, sir?**

(A) No, I have no other appointments.

(B) Really? What did he say?

(C) Of course. You deserve it.

30. **What time shall I come back here to meet the representative?**

(A) How abut noon, sir?

(B) Sure, tomorrow sounds fine.

(C) Maybe tomorrow will be late.

Chapter 3 Social Network Service

Dialogue Challenge 3

Karl : Hi, Janet, how are you doing?

Janet : I'm doing good and you Karl?

Karl : I'm quite well. Thank you. I have a question for you. Are you using Facebook?

Janet : Yes, I am a big fan of Facebook. but I really do not check very often.

Karl : I see. And then, how often do you check Facebook?

Janet : I am trying to check it at leat twice a week.

Karl : Understandable. I used to be on Facebook so many times before. I was trying to catch up with everybody on Facebook. But then I came to know that I was consuming so much of precious time.

I don't want to lose my time, since I should use my time for the productive activities such as studying, working out, doing homework. It is important to communicate with other people, in that we are living in the era of information and communication. Actually I am afraid I can lose the ties and connection with people around me when I disconnect Facebook.

Janet : Facebook has really become a big social network service. When you disconnect it, you can get lost from what is actually happening around you, in the country, and the world right now. But what is important is that you should control your life yourself. When you are overwhelmed by Facebook and you are occupied with the burden of the use, you need to get a rest from it to adjust your life and your time. Facebook is not everything for you. Remember that you are the master of your life.

Karl : Thank you for your advice, Janet. You seem to be a guru in my life.

Janet : You're just kidding. I am not your mentor, but I really want you to live your life well. Just command your life, Karl. You are the captain of your life to sail over the troubled sea. You open a path through and cope with the rugged world.

Karl : Thank you, Janet. You're right. I should live my life.

Sentence Challenge 3

01. I am a big fan of Facebook.

02. I am trying to check it at leat twice a week.

03. I used to be on Facebook so many times before.

04. I came to know that I was consuming so much of precious time.

05. I don't want to lose my time, since I should use my time for the productive activities.

06. It is important to communicate with other people, in that we are living in the era of information and communication.

07. Facebook has really become a big social network service.

08. You need to get a rest from it to adjust your life and your time.

09. You seem to be a guru in my life.

10. You are the captain of your life to sail over the troubled sea.

11. You open a path through and cope with the rugged world.

Grammar Challenge 3

How about + (verb-ing)

You're asking someone their opinions on something or if they would like to do something.

Here are some examples:

"How about hiking?"
"How about drinking with me?"
"How about changing the sofa in the living room?"
"How about donating our asset?"
"How about going to the movies this weekend?"
"How about going to the gym for your health?"
"How about using mobile banking?"
"How about opening a new account of the mail?"
"How about singing a song for me?"
"How about making a good impression for the customers?"

Paragraph Challenge 3

Questions 1–4 refer to the following paragraph.

The Metropolitan Messenger is an independent community newspaper that has 1.______ for the residents of Boston for over 130 years. All of our articles are 2.________ by the journalists employed by the Metropolitan Messenger. Copies of the Metropolitan Messenger are also 3.________ at the City Hall, Town Cafe, and almost every convenient store in the county. Any articles or photographs that are used in the newspapers reserve the copy rights. Especially articles from the Metropolitan Messenger will be available at the 4.________ of every week by papers and electronically.

01.
(A) served
(B) participated
(C) called
(D) represented

02.
(A) writers
(B) wrote
(C) writing
(D) written

03. (A) avail
(B) available
(C) avails
(D) availing

04. (A) begin
(B) beginners
(C) begins
(D) beginning

Conversation Challenge 3

01. **When will you release the marketable smart phone, Mr. Johnson?**

(A) At the office.

(B) This upcoming Thursday, I believe.

(C) The last time I saw you.

02. **Do you know why my reserved air ticket has been canceled?**

(A) Because you mJanet a phone call of cancelation last week

(B) Yes, I can cancel it.

(C) It's not far from LA.

03. **Where did you purchase the long goose jacket?**

(A) Only 10 bucks

(B) For Canada

(C) From the internet shopping mall.

04. **We are running out of gas, is there any gas station near here?**

(A) Yes, it is located two blocks away from where we are.

(B) The station's very busy.

(C) I will run this evening for my health.

05. **How many people attended the party?**

(A) At least 100 gallons.

(B) He's the party animal.

(C) It is countless.

06. **Can you tell me the way to the Central station?**

(A) About 20 minutes.

(B) I need to go to the station.

(C) Take the bus number 511.

07. **Where is an ATM in the precinct?**

(A) Anytime in the afternoon.

(B) No, ATM doesn't mean Automatic Trans Mission.

(C) In front of the department of accounting.

08. **We are not supposed to use internet at work, why?**

(A) The maintenance staff.

(B) To prevent a thief

(C) That is the order of the boss.

09. **When do you expect we can finish up the project?**

(A) The same finisher

(B) You are not expecting

(C) At least at the beginning of next month.

10. **Will you give me a hand when I move the plant to the department of personnel?**

(A) I'd love to.

(B) Don't worry. I will not be there.

(C) Right when you are free.

11. **Can you imagine that we are not going to get a pay raise?**

(A) A full-time service

(B) At the bottom of the ground

(C) Don't worry. the boss promised to increase our salary.

12. **When can we get a maintenance service for the copier?**

(A) In about two hours

(B) I'm not maintain the department.

(C) Service is not good enough.

13. **Your wife is expecting your baby next month, isn't she?**

(A) Right, how did you know that?

(B) I love a baby.

(C) Expectation is limited.

14. **I'd like to make a reservation of air ticket for Boston.**

(A) Boston is far away from here.

(B) An airline is bankrupted.

(C) No, problem. Let me help you sir.

15. **How do you get to work by car pool or by train?**

(A) We share a ride for the purpose of energy saving.

(B) That doesn't work very well.

(C) Train is not leaving now.

16. **When will you make a presentation for the project?**

(A) Tomorrow, you should be attendant.

(B) The presentation will not be long.

(C) I can handle the project.

17. **Our company is looking for an excellent designer of the outdoor fashion.**

(A) About 10 percent discount

(B) I heard that news.

(C) Didn't you have it designed?

18. **Are you on Facebook, when are you free?**

(A) I don't know it much.

(B) She posts a lot of photos on it.

(C) Yes, when I am not busy.

19. **Please be careful not to catch a cold, it is frigid outside.**

(A) You can have a seat outside.

(B) Thank you, I hate the cold weather.

(C) OK, we will carefully deal with the frozen meat.

20. **Who is the representative of the customer service satisfaction department?**

(A) Mr. John is in charge of it.

(B) They are not representing the company.

(C) I can be satisfied with it.

21. **Do we have to post an opening at the classified ads right now?**

(A) I waited for the new comers.

(B) Maybe, we will hire him.

(C) No, it isn't necessary.

22. **Where can I get the information concerning your article?**

(A) Another a couple of hours

(B) Call him right now.

(C) From my office

23. **I have a medical checkup today, what should be watched out?**

(A) I'm a medical doctor.

(B) Don't drink even water.

(C) We watched him recently.

24. **How much is the courier service?**

(A) It depends on the weight of package.

(B) I can serve you right now.

(C) No, it isn't not expensive.

25. **Why do I have to clean up the sink at the lab?**

(A) Yes, I hope to use the lab.

(B) For the next person to use

(C) They're going to clean the lab.

26. **How about the production line of the smart phones?**

(A) It is going well right now.

(B) The smart phones are expensive.

(C) A production line is located on the second floor.

27. **Would you like another cup of coffee?**

(A) At the coffee shop

(B) I'd love to

(C) I will order right now.

28. **Why don't you use the new software, Daven?**

(A) I can't afford it.

(B) It is not expensive.

(C) Every software is worth it.

29. **When is the presentation for the new users of the released game?**

(A) I should present it.

(B) They'll need the new games.

(C) It has been postponed until next month.

30. **Why were you late for joining our company?**

(A) Because I didn't finish up my graduate degree.

(B) I have another appointment.

(C) A few weeks later

Chapter 4 Dream Job

Dialogue Challenge 4

Janet : So Karl, did you like your first job?

Karl : Actually when I got a job. I was 14 years old. My parents wanted me to have a part time job to experience a bit of the jungle of the world. They persuaded me at the early age to get a working experience which can be worked as something like the preventive vaccination. But unluckily the manager at the local diner dismissed me after a month of my working due to the employment law to restrict minors who are not in the working age.

Janet : Do you mean by that you worked illegally despite your younger age?

Karl : Yeah, sort of. Firstly I didn't know that 14 year-old person can't get a job.

In New York State, minors can get a job when they are 15 and over. I was ignorant of employment law in New York. Even a manager didn't know the rules exactly. But later on he told me I could not work any more, after consulting a lawyer for his business.

Janet : But you were great. You had the experience of working at the age of fourteen. Weren't your working at a Radio Shack after that?

Karl : Yeah, it's true. I could get a lot of fun when I worked for a Radio Shack at Binghamton. I am a computer lover. I dealt with computer stuffs, and a lot of electronic gadgetry and equipment.

Janet : I know. The Radio Shack is famous for its electronic goods. I opened my smart phone at a Radio Shack near my home in the Riverdale County. I could get over 30 percent discount from my monthly calling fee. I was lucky to find a credit card to save the fee with the use of it. They only charged me 20 dollars a month from the original bill of 30 dollars. We should be smart when we use the smart phones.

Karl : Yes, it makes sense. I thought you were a nerd, but you turned out to be a genius to save money.

Janet : Thank you for your compliment. Do you want me to help you to have a cheap smart phone?

Karl : No thank you. I can handle my own stuffs. But your consideration will be much appreciated.

Sentence Challenge 4

01. My parents wanted me to have a part time job to experience a bit of the jungle of the world.

02. They persuaded me at the early age to get a working experience which can be worked as something like the preventive vaccination.

03. Unluckily the manager at the local diner dismissed me after a month of my working due to the employment law to restrict minors who are not in the working age.

04. Do you mean by that you worked illegally despite of your younger age?

05. In New York State, minors can get a job when they are 15 and over.

06. Even a manager didn't know the rules

07. Later on he told me I could not work any more, after consulting a lawyer for his business.

08. You had the experience of working at the age of fourteen.

09. Weren't your working at a Radio Shack after that?

10. I am a computer lover. I dealt with computer stuffs, and a lot of electronic gadgetry and equipment.

11. Radio Shack is famous for its electronic goods.

12. I could get over 30 percent discount from my monthly calling fee. I was lucky to find a credit card to save the fee with the use of it.

13. They only charged me 20 dollars a month from the original bill of 30 dollars.

Grammar Challenge 4

I would like to + (verb)

This expression lets the listeners to know the intent and interest of the speakers during the conversation.

Here are some examples:

"I would like to know the whole truth."

"I would like to tell you the story next time."

"I would like to have my summer vacation earlier."

"I would like to invite you home tonight."

"I would like to investigate into the case."

"I would like to become a professor someday."

"I would like to check my Facebook."

"I would like to appreciate your kindness."

"I would like to learn more languages."

"I would like to have a talk with you."

Paragraph Challenge 4

Questions 1–4 refer to the following paragraph.

This is to let you know that during the Thanksgiving holidays, we will be 1.______ discounted sales items in every Radio Shack store. For this event you should bring the coupons from the Daily Rivervill which is our weekly 2.________ in the county. During the holidays you can purchase the electronic goods 3._____ a remarkably cheap price. Please do not lose the big chance for 4.______ your money during the holiday season.

01. (A) offering
(B) have offering
(C) accepting
(D) accepted

02. (A) newer
(B) books
(C) newspaper
(D) notebooks

03. (A) at
(B) before
(C) beyond
(D) due

04. (A) save
(B) saving
(C) saves
(D) saver

Conversation Challenge 4

01. How many people did attend the seminar at the University of Tulsa?

(A) Let's meet at the university.

(B) It was a good seminar

(C) Almost 100 students

02. What kinds of kitchen stuffs does your company make?

(A) Especially stoves

(B) The production line makes

(C) Yes, I like the kitchen work.

03. How can I order the food at this diner?

(A) No thank you, I'll have some later.

(B) It's a new diner.

(C) Please, push the button on the table.

04. **How can I reach an ATM from here?**

(A) Just walk to the student hall.

(B) Yes, I have an ATM

(C) That's a large ATM.

05. **When do you think I can see your boss?**

(A) Maybe you are right.

(B) My boss is a good gentleman.

(C) Just after the lunch time

06. **Do you know who wants to have the fax machine fixed?**

(A) I should have my fax.

(B) The boss of our company

(C) Thanks, that's a good idea.

07. **Do you prefer to leave the office now or later?**

(A) It's quite preferable.

(B) I'm good now.

(C) I'd better leave in two hours.

08. **Do you happen to know the route 110?**

(A) Across a small bridge.

(B) Sure, go straight, and turn right at the intersection.

(C) You could lower it a little bit.

09. **How can I reach the lab in Johnson and Johnson?**

(A) It is not within my reach.

(B) An yearly leave will be fine.

(C) After getting a permission front desk, use the elevator.

10. **Where can I find your company in the Jackson County?**

(A) Where is the counter?

(B) You can give me a call at the airport, and I will pick you up.

(C) Have you checked the my desk?

11. **I am really happy to get a concert ticket of One Direction.**

(A) I am happy, too.

(B) One direction is sometimes dangerous.

(C) I need to go to get some directions.

12. **When can we talk about the crucial issue of dismissal?**

(A) No, discussion is not required tomorrow.

(B) Just after the board meeting

(C) I would like to talk about it.

13. **When do you open the grocery shop?**

(A) It's close to my grocery store.

(B) At a different shop

(C) Every day at 9:00 a.m.

14. **Do you want me to bring the finished report today or tomorrow?**

(A) Anytime you are free.

(B) Not in my life time

(C) He finished it very early.

15. **How can we satisfy the new customers?**

(A) I'll put satisfy him.

(B) Quality is the best strategy.

(C) New comers were late.

16. **Do you mind opening the window for the fresh air?**

(A) No, go ahead. It's very stuffy in here.

(B) Thank you for changing windows.

(C) The orange is not fresh in the room.

17. **Who is the designer of the new building?**

(A) OK, we'll design it soon.

(B) An architecture in our development department

(C) Just sign to get the building.

18. **Would you like to visit me tomorrow? I am busy right now.**

(A) No, our office is closed.

(B) I'd love to. I will come here again.

(C) What do you mean by that?

19. **How often do you meet your boss?**

(A) Once in a day I see him to report the sales figures.

(B) It's in the meeting room.

(C) I haven't had a meal yet.

20. **Has the research scientist's flight been delayed?**

(A) Has he signed off on it?

(B) I can look up this status on my phone.

(C) He specializes in ancient Greek languages.

21. **Who's in charge of building the new tower?**

(A) Until August 30th.

(B) Mike is not leaving today.

(C) My senior manager

22. **Are you interested in the new opening in my company?**

(A) Sure, how do I send the email to your company?

(B) They are not interested in it.

(C) We already opened it.

23. **Our newly launched project is going well, isn't it?**

(A) Definitely yes.

(B) Every project is not easy.

(C) It was a new event.

24. **Are you satisfying with your pay?**

(A) No, I want it to be increased.

(B) The payroll is dealt with Mrs. Kempton.

(C) After I pay for it.

25. **Does the front desk know you are a new comer?**

(A) A new comer should be careful all the time.

(B) The front des is always busy.

(C) No, I told them several times, but they don't recognize me.

26. **Can I get the new brochures for the concert?**

(A) Sure, I'll go to the concert.

(B) It's a new brochure.

(C) Yes, just pick them up at the front desk.

27. **Do you know what time the meeting will be finished?**

(A) At around 9 p.m.

(B) Yes, I have met him.

(C) The team will finish the project soon.

28. **Excuse me, Doctor, when do you want me to see you again?**

(A) See you again when I am free
(B) At the hall
(C) Just when you have your sore back again.

29. **Who is the best person for the position?**

(A) The position is not opened yet.
(B) Mr. Jason Geeambee
(C) Thanks, I can take care of it.

30. **Does your boss want you to leave your company now?**

(A) It's very convenient.
(B) I'm not sure. but he is mad at my poor performance.
(C) I will stay for the night.

Chapter 5 Wedding

Dialogue Challenge 5

Janet : Hi, Karl. We are talking about the wedding ceremony. Did you get much stress from it?

Karl : Yes, Indeed. It was awfully stressful in many ways. Firstly, I lost the personal identification number for my bank account. It was very critical for me to draw money from the account. But nothing came to my mind concerning the PIN. I had no choice but to reset the PIN. It took a whole day for me to correct my bank account. When the PIN slipped my mind, I got embarrassed too much.

Janet : I can understand your suffering and stress. Actually I had the same kind of experience before. It might be different, but from the point that I was too much embarrassed, you would figure out my situation, too. Two years ago, I lost my wallet at a public restroom in the metropolitan subway in Seoul. When I reached home I could remember the noise of something had been dropped by a toilet. I went urgently back to the restroom to find my wallet. But I could not find it. It was a really frustrating and heart breaking experience at the scene. I doubted that someone picked it up and disappeared. But after a while I went to the Lost and Found. An officer there gave my wallet back after checking my identification.

Karl : How did you prove your identification before the officer? How did the officer come to know that you were the owner of the wallet?

Janet : Thank God, I had my student ID in my pocket not in the wallet. And I showed him my ID. He asked me how much money in the wallet. And then I answered that the officer could find out five ten-dollar bills in the wallet. He asked me my exact address. I could answer for the question very easily. Everything went well after the exact answer for the amount of money and my address.

Karl : You were lucky at that time, Janet. I think we should have some memos for our PIN just in case.

Janet : Right, do not believe in your brain, but be careful with the loss of memos holding crucial information like the PIN. You'd better try to memorize the PIN instead of writing it down on the papers.

Karl : Thank you for your tips. Let me give it a shot to memorize it.

Sentence Challenge 5

01. Did you get much stress from it?

02. It was awfully stressful in many ways.

03. I lost the personal identification number for my bank account.

04. It was very critical for me to draw money from the account.

05. Nothing came to my mind concerning the PIN.

06. I had no choice but to reset the PIN.

07. It took a whole day for me to correct my bank account.

08. The PIN slipped my mind.

09. I can understand your suffering and stress.

10. I went urgently back to the restroom to find my wallet.

11. It was a really frustrating and heart breaking experience at the scene.

12. I doubted that someone picked it up and disappeared.

13. How did you prove your identification before the officer?

14. How did the officer come to know that you were the owner of the wallet?

15. You'd better try to memorize the PIN instead of writing it down on the papers.

16. Let me give it a shot to memorize it.

Grammar Challenge 5

I feel like + (verb-ing)

The phrase can be used when you are expressing your feeling and intent to do something in a certain situation.

Here are some examples:

"I feel like traveling the whole world."

"I feel like going to the amusement park."

"I feel like seeing you soon."

"I feel like eating a slice of pizza right now."

"I feel like singing a Christmas song."

"I feel like having a good meal with you."

"I feel like listening to the cheerful music."

Paragraph Challenge 5

Questions 1–4 refer to the following paragraph.

You should be notified that next year we are going to 1.______the tag price of the winter outfits. We are 2.______ pressure from the risen cost in manufacturing winter jackets and trench coats mainly due to the expensive imported clothing materials. The tariffs for the clothing material have been risen up to 10 % 3. ______ to those of last year. Hopefully you will understand the hardship of our company is facing now. You can contact our sales department anytime to consult the quality and 4.______ of our winter outfits. Thank you.

01. (A) increase
(B) riser
(C) rising
(D) increasing

02. (A) get
(B) getting
(C) gotten
(D) gets

03. (A) compared
(B) comes
(C) comparison
(D) coming

04. (A) much
(B) quantity
(C) many
(D) block

Conversation Challenge 5

01. **Why don't we leave a week earlier so we can buy a cheeper ticket?**

(A) Yes, they were earlier than we expected.
(B) I'm leaving by the theater.
(C) Good idea. I'll check the prices tomorrow.

02. **Have the mechanics finished fixing the plant equipment?**

(A) Yes, they had their job done, sir.
(B) I don't think she's finished.
(C) I haven't decided when to plant them.

03. **Who's going to replace the broken copier?**

(A) I called the mechanic who can take care of it.
(B) Yes, he was paying with it.
(C) The window was broken.

04. **You found an apartment to rent, didn't you?**

(A) Yes, in the down town yesterday

(B) Unfortunately , I'm still using it.

(C) Yes, I lent it to my customer.

05. **Would you like to join the annual party for the company?**

(A) No, I don't like to go to the doctor's.

(B) Sure, I go to the party all the time.

(C) Actually, I was not in there.

06. **What did you say to Allan Karlson?**

(A) I just asked him whether he was good or not.

(B) No, he didn't know what he said.

(C) At the front desk.

07. **How are you going to get the Grand Central Park from here?**

(A) I should be there by 9:30.

(B) I'll take a taxi to get there.

(C) Yes, I'll start to work next day.

08. **Aren't you moving tomorrow, Mr. Parkerson?**

(A) No, I bought the tables last week.

(B) Yes, but I need the extra money.

(C) No, not until I can find out another place.

09. **Where's the office of the chairman in this building?**

(A) At the 11th floor

(B) The head master will bring you a menu, sir.

(C) There's nobody in this building.

10. **Why were you late for the luncheon today?**

(A) Because he couldn't change the form.

(B) No, he wasn't able to make the change.

(C) I am sorry, due to the traffic jam.

11. **Would you like to have your dessert right now, sir?**

(A) I think I've seen enough for the day.

(B) No, not right now after enjoying the main plate.

(C) I think I can wait to taste the dessert tomorrow.

12. **When do you think the notebook will be mended?**

(A) The man will keep your notebook.

(B) They'll have it mended.

(C) When the mechanic finishes his job for it.

13. **Do you want to take a break right now or later?**

(A) I have some problems with the brakes.

(B) I'm sorry, I didn't mean to break it.

(C) I am really tired. Let's have it at the moment.

14. **How about playing tennis this weekend, Barbie?**

(A) No, I played there last week.

(B) My wife and I are going out tonight.

(C) It sounds perfect.

15. **How about retiring from your company?**

(A) I haven't heard anything yet.

(B) No, it's not an emergency.

(C) No way, I can work for the company until I am 80.

16. **Do you remember that we are going to have a date tomorrow?**

(A) Sorry, but I already had a date.

(B) Absolutely, I am expecting it.

(C) What are you doing right now?

17. **Can I take a look at your sales report, Mrs. Camelia?**

(A) In a minute, it will be put your desk, sir.

(B) The sales doesn't go well.

(C) Sure, you can examine the sales team.

18. **Where do you want to go for your summer leave?**

(A) The summer leave is very short.

(B) I am going nowhere. Let me catch some sleep.

(C) We spent a week for the summer leave.

19. **Could you get me a few copies for this page?**

(A) Sure, I'll do it right now.

(B) No, I didn't get copies.

(C) I don't think I can fix the copier.

20. **How much is installing the solar panels?**

(A) The ones I bought last year were broken

(B) Yes, the panel is ready to talk about it.

(C) It depends on how large those are.

21. **Who is going to handle the problems of budgeting?**

(A) Yes, the law firm of Parkersons will take care of it.

(B) No decision has been mJanet yet.

(C) The department of planning and budget

22. **Are you planning to travel Italy this week?**

(A) Yes, how did you know that?

(B) The last two weeks for Italy.

(C) It's such a beautiful time for sightseeing.

23. **Do you think that we should have the written statement?**

(A) I also think he is right.

(B) That may be wrong to think about it.

(C) Yes, just for the case of any problems

24. **Do you know the reason of cancelling the seminar.**

(A) Something came up due to the severe weather

(B) No, I can cancel it.

(C) I know we should attend the seminar.

25. **Is smoking allowed in here? Mr. Dennison?**

(A) Yes, it is the point for you.

(B) No, I stayed in the room and did not smoke there.

(C) Yes, the allowance is not enough.

26. **What are you going to do for your living?**

(A) We are not living until 100.

(B) Yes, living isn't easy.

(C) Don't worry. I have an enough pension.

27. **I heard your company was suffering from the huge deficit.**

(A) No, we don't have any money.

(B) Yes, but we already got over it.

(C) Yes, we have a big company.

28. **Did you have any locker in this building?**

(A) Yes, but you should get the permission from the maintenance department for the use of it.

(B) Not in my yard

(C) Right after they locked the door.

29. **When do you want to have your test? now or tomorrow?**

(A) Yes, I think you are right.

(B) I would do it right now.

(C) Tomorrow is much better for me.

30. **Why don't we have steak at the fancy diner in the down town?**

(A) I am sorry, I am out of the budget this week.

(B) You have a good dine.

(C) Yes, we are late for the diner.

Chapter 6 Bakery

Dialogue Challenge 6

Karl : Hi, Janet. I hear that you're a professional baker. Do you like your job?

Janet : Yeah. I really like to bake. It's pretty exciting to make bakery products. You will know that a bakery produces and sells flour-based food baked in an oven such as bread, cookies, cakes, pastries, and pies. Nowadays, retail bakeries in the town sell coffee and tea together for the customers who want to have baked goods at the shops. There are famous international brands like Muffin Break and Wonder Bread. I had worked as a baker at one franchise of Muffin Break in L.A. I could have the precious career from Muffin Break.

Karl : Do you think being a baker is your dream job?

Janet : My dream when I was young was to be a doctor. But it had been changed.
I can have a really good time when I touch and make a shape with dough.

It is lot of fun to me. Additionally I really like to eat cookies. I can enjoy them as much as I want. But I am careful with taking sweet stuffs, since I am suffering from the disease of diabetes.

Karl : Oh, I am sorry to hear that. You should control when you taking sweet or sweetened food for your health. And then what kinds of ingredients do you like to use?

Janet : As you know, a variety of ingredients can be used for the bakery. Well, Chocolate, milk, egg, butter, are basic ingredients for the bakery. But I like to use organic cheese nowadays.

Karl : Do you have any special recipe for making good bread or cookies?

Janet : For the special bread, I have the recipe inherited from my great grand mother. Dissolve yeast in warm water. Add honey, and stir well. Mix in whole wheat flour, salt, and vegetable oil. It looks quite easy. But the temperature of an oven is very essential. That is the top secret.

Karl : Wow, it's great. Someday, let me try to taste your special bread. My mouth is watering now.

Janet : Come and eat the bread when you are off from your work and free.

Karl : Thank you for your kindness and affection.

Sentence Challenge 6

01. I hear that you're a professional baker.

02. You will know that a bakery produces and sells flour-based food baked in an oven such as bread, cookies, cakes, pastries, and pies.

03. There are famous international brands like Muffin Break and Wonder Bread.

04. I had worked as a baker at one franchise of Muffin Break in L.A.

05. My dream when I was young was to be a doctor.

06. I can enjoy them as much as I want.

07. But I am careful with taking sweet stuffs, since I am suffering from the disease of diabetes.

08. You should control when you taking sweet or sweetened food for your health.

09. What kinds of ingredients do you like to use?

10. As you know, a variety of ingredients can be used for the bakery. Well,

11. Do you have any special recipe for making good bread or cookies?

12. I have the recipe inherited from my great grand mother.

13. Someday, let me try to taste your special bread.

14. My mouthis watering now.

Grammar Challenge 6

I think I should + (verb)

You are saying that you have a strong intention about doing a particular action.

Here are some examples:

"I think I should work out every day."

"I think I should take a rest."

"I think I should go to bed."

"I think I should work hard for the Mid-term."

"I think I should go right now."

When you want to express your intention not doing something, you can use don't or doesn't.

Here are some examples:

"I do not think I should go out now."

"I do not think I should tell you the truth."

"I do not think I should buy the expensive shirt."

"I do not think I should walk my dog."

"I do not think I should drive a car when I take a cold medicine."

Paragraph Challenge 6

Questions 1–4 refer to the following paragraph.

Beginning on Nov. 1st, we will be using a new banking service that will 1.______ your bank account. First, your online and mobile banking will be 2.______ temporarily from Oct.30 to Oct. 31st. Be careful when you use your electronic banking on those days. Second, You should 3.________ the newly reinforced security program for your secured banking. Thank you in advance 4______ your cooperation and understanding.

01. (A) affecting
(B) affectionate
(C) affect
(D) affection

02. (A) closed
(B) correct
(C) reject
(D) entered

03. (A) down
(B) download
(C) disturb
(D) distributing

04. (A) for
(B) after
(C) before
(D) between

Conversation Challenge 6

01. **Where are you going to take Mr. Johnson out to lunch?**

(A) At 3:30

(B) No, he has another appointment.

(C) To a fancy restaurant.

02. **Are you going to leave for New York?**

(A) No, it's too expensive.

(B) Yes, it is my fist time to go there.

(C) I should make it on time.

03. **I am sorry to interrupt you but would you like me to help you?**

(A) Yes, it is busy.

(B) No, I didn't give him my thought

(C) No, thank you. That's all right.

04. **That milk in the refrigerator doesn't look very fresh, does it?**

(A) I would agree.

(B) He doesn't it meat.

(C) Yes, it does.

05. **What will you do this afternoon, Mrs Kate?**

(A) They want to postpone the meeting until tomorrow.

(B) Well, I have no plans right now.

(C) They will do it on that side.

06. **How many board members are coming to the meeting?**

(A) Yes, many people are shopping there.

(B) Only 5 of them

(C) I bought them through my stockbroker.

07. **Is the copy machine working well now?**

(A) Because I am cone using it.

(B) No, it should be taken care of by a mechanic.

(C) No, he wasn't able to get it done.

08. **How much is the rate of this package, Mrs. Hellen?**

(A) No, I put them on the floor.

(B) Mary set then on her desk.

(C) Sorry, I don't know it yet.

09. **Why don't we have a fresh air and break?**

(A) Because the car was going to fast.

(B) Yeah, I need some fresh air.

(C) Yes, it is a good idea.

10. **What are you going to do in the near future?**

(A) I want to have my own business in two years.

(B) I have to fly over to Disney Land.

(C) Yes, that plan does look good.

11. **How can I get to the new airport in New York?**

(A) Yes, you should be able to.

(B) You'd better take a taxi.

(C) No, I want to stay in New York.

12. **Did you get your car fixed yesterday?**

(A) I put it under my car.

(B) No, I could not make an arrangement for it.

(C) Yes, they did not fix it.

13. **How are you doing these days, Mr. Parkerson?**

(A) I am quite good, thank you.

(B) No, I'll go the day after tomorrow.

(C) Terribly sorry about that.

14. **When is your doctor's appointment, Mr. Kensington?**

(A) At that new clinic downstairs.

(B) No, it isn't.

(C) At 2:30 today

15. **You haven't sent out my parcel yet, have you?**

(A) Don't worry. It is delivered by the courier service.

(B) Yes, it does smell nice, doesn't it?

(C) No, I don't have to.

16. **Who will take over your job when you leave your company?**

(A) It is not decided yet.

(B) It hasn't been late.

(C) Mark Brown is moving now.

17. **Do you need the report to be done tomorrow, boss?**

(A) Who know?

(B) We need not your boss.

(C) I'd like it today if it is possible.

18. **Could you tell me the way to the forest in the Central Park?**

(A) Absolutely, go strait from the intersection.

(B) I wasn't able to go the park.

(C) Yes, I already put in the park.

19. **How much longer do I have to wait in line for the concert?**

(A) I only have to go for two blocs for the concert.

(B) In about 20 minutes

(C) He wants me to reduce the line.

20. **What are you going to do when you have your leave?**

(A) That the leave isn't long enough.

(B) I haven't decided yet.

(C) No, I don't think it right.

21. **Where can I get my notebook fixed?**

(A) Yes, you can fix it.

(B) At the after sales service center

(C) She doesn't like notebooks.

22. **How do you like your new company, Johnson?**

(A) Oh, it's the best apartment.

(B) I wish I still had my former job.

(C) I have a great time.

23. **What time do you want me to pick you up at the airport, Karl?**

(A) Yes, I think I have time.

(B) Around 7:00 PM

(C) Yes, could you please?

24. **How about your marketing job, Mr. Delkerson?**

(A) Until now, it is good.

(B) It's usually done for marketing.

(C) Yes, he was a marketer.

25. **How come you have spent so much money last month?**

(A) Yes, that was much money.

(B) I had a big loss in the stock market.

(C) She had spent money.

26. **When do you think I should take a picture?**

(A) Right after the show

(B) I think you should not draw a picture.

(C) Let me decide to take a picture.

27. **Are you tired, Mrs. Dolton? You look so shabby.**

(A) Yes, they were all tired.

(B) Yes, I could not catch a sleep last night.

(C) No, I still feel tired.

28. **That dinner was really fantastic in honor of Mrs. Peterson.**

(A) Yes, I enjoyed it very much.

(B) No, it's wrong to talk about her honor.

(C) Yes, she was quite good.

29. **Can you speak other languages except English?**

(A) I can't. I just command only English.

(B) Yes, they speak English.

(C) Only a little bit.

30. **Fill out this form for your medical checkup.**

(A) Yes, I will do it right now.

(B) How much is it?

(C) Sorry, we don't have anymore checkup for you.

Chapter 7 Technology

Dialogue Challenge 7

Janet : We are living in the era of state of the art. I want to buy a smart watch.

Karl : When it comes to a smart watch. Some people take it as just an accessory.

But it can tell the time, and can beam important notifications connected with the smart phone. The problem is that it is too expensive.

Janet : Yeah, it is the hard reality. But it is very much convenient. What's more impressive is that many of today's recent models can also perform a ton of novel tricks, such as enabling you to search the internet with your voice, tracking your exercise with GPS.

Karl : Actually, I am using an Apple smart watch. It costed me an arm and a leg. It was very much expensive.

Janet : The company says that the Apple is the best smart watch you can buy right now. But I don't think it is right. I am not a picky person, but it is the exaggeration of the features of the gadget.

Karl : For me, an Apple smart watch really performs well with the connection of the phone with the speed of LTE. But the problem is that it drains the battery soon.

Janet : I heard the non-LTE version does not use much electricity, offering much longer battery life and it is a lot cheaper than the premium LTE version.
Also it is easy to upgrade.

Karl : What I like is that it is stunning to boot. I know it is absolutely a fancy gadget in the era of cutting edge technology.

Janet : I heard the technology of smart phones is compared to that of launching a space shuttle into the orbit of the universe.

Karl : I can't imagine our life in 100 years. Can we live in the Mars?

Sentence Challenge 7

01. We are living in the era of state of the art.

02. It can beam important notifications connected with the smart phone.

03. What's more impressive is that many of today's recent models can also perform a ton of novel tricks.

04. It costed me an arm and a leg.

05. I am not a picky person.

06. The problem is that it drains the battery soon.

07. I heard the non-LTE version does not use much electricity, offering much longer battery life

08. It is a lot cheaper than the premium LTE version.

09. I know it is absolutely a fancy gadget in the era of cutting edge technology.

10. I heard the technology of smart phones is compared to that of launching a space shuttle into the orbit of the universe.

11. I can't imagine our life in 100 years.

12. Can we live in the Mars?

Grammar Challenge 7

You're supposed to + (verb)

When you say 'You're', it is a contraction of the words 'you are.' When you use 'You're' with the words 'supposed to' you are making a suggestion should be happened.

Here are some examples:

"You're supposed to tell me the truth."
"You're supposed to leave the office at 6 p.m."
"You're supposed to follow my advice."
"You're supposed to apply for the company."
"You're supposed to pay the bill instead of her."
"You are supposed to calm down."
"You are supposed to drive safe in wet weather."
"You are supposed to take the cold medicine."
"You are supposed to see a doctor today."
"You are supposed to leave me alone."

Paragraph Challenge 7

Questions 1–4 refer to the following paragraph.

You are receiving the e–mail concerning the 1.________ of a password change for your T band for MK Teleservice. Your 2.______ has been settled again, and you should change your password. Please be notified that it will 3._______ at least one hour or so for the total change. Log on to www. mkteleservice. com. Please complete the form, and change your password according to the 4.__________ given on the page. Thank you all the time for your loyalty and long–term use of our service.

01. (A) request
(B) requested
(C) requesting
(D) requests

02. (A) account
(B) accountant
(C) accounts
(D) accountable

03. (A) taken
(B) taking
(C) took
(D) take

04. (A) induction
(B) introduction
(C) intake
(D) instructions

Conversation Challenge 7

01. What is the special menu at this diner?

(A) Yes, I've had enough dinner.

(B) Good idea.

(C) Meat pasta with cheese, sir

02. How long do I have to wait for your new book?

(A) It was am hour ago.

(B) It will take at least two more days

(C) I think you books are interesting.

03. Do you know where the restroom is in this precinct?

(A) The rest rooms are full of people.

(B) There is one outside this building.

(C) You can rest in that chair.

04. **Can you notify me when you can complete this project?**

(A) No, I haven't finished it yet.

(B) I started on it yesterday.

(C) By the end of the week.

05. **Do you want to grab a bite to eat with me, Jackson?**

(A) Don't pull so hard.

(B) That sounds perfect!

(C) I think it's fish and chips.

06. **How many pages for the new website are you preparing?**

(A) I plan to page it now.

(B) More than 20

(C) I thought it was pretty prepared.

07. **How do you come to your office, do you drive yourself?**

(A) Yes, I will get my driver's license next month.

(B) Actually, I commute by subway

(C) The bus is not probably faster than the metro.

08. **How did you find out the new client for the company?**

(A) It depends on where you want to see the client.

(B) It is the result of my trial to contact latent customers.

(C) We'll need the company.

09. **When is the anniversary of your company?**

(A) Today is the day.

(B) It's downtown Norton Road 13th.

(C) Next month, he will celebrate his birthday.

10. **What do you want for your dish of lunch?**

(A) Oil Pane pasta

(B) We wash the dish all the time.

(C) They said it was not lunch time.

11. **Would you tell me how shipping fees are charged, Mr. Markerson?**

(A) How much are they?

(B) It depends on the weight as far as I know.

(C) Wrap this item separately, please.

12. **David, do we have any problems with the network connectivity?**

(A) Yes, I'm living alone.

(B) The online is closed today.

(C) I am leaving at 6:00.

13. **How do you calculate population in the region near San Francisco?**

(A) By the measurement provided by Indexon company

(B) It's a casual affair.

(C) No, I am not going to the fair.

14. **Would you mind using your mobile phone for a moment?**

(A) No, I haven't used it.

(B) I'm sorry, it is now out of electricity.

(C) Don't mind about the use.

15. **How do you contact your boss when he is out of town?**

(A) The boss calls me when he needs.

(B) The boss's looking forward to her trip to New York.

(C) I think the boss was busy.

16. **What is your preference on the choice of your jacket?**

(A) It's my favorite color.

(B) The late comer is not chooser.

(C) I like red color of it.

17. **Where do you want to go for dinner, Meggy?**

(A) I want to go to Mandarine Diner

(B) I'm going to dine now.

(C) The dinner is expensive, Meg

18. **What are you going to take metro or a taxi?**

(A) I love training every day.

(B) My preference is my car.

(C) Yes, I walked to the station.

19. **Have you met our new client, Mrs. Melanie?**

(A) Yes, we had a meeting already.

(B) Yes, I live with a client.

(C) No, I am not meeting you anymore.

20. **Who was in charge of completing the new project?**

(A) Mr. Jackson is the head of it.

(B) They completed their mission.

(C) The charge is ten dollars.

21. **When do you expect they can give a hand on the project?**

(A) I actually thought it was handy.

(B) By the end of this week, maybe.

(C) I think we can give him a thought.

22. **Are you supposed to meet our managing director, Malcom?**

(A) I've never met Malcom.

(B) No, I don't know him.

(C) Actually, the meeting was cancelled.

23. **They could not get in touch with the new comers, do you know the reason?**

(A) I was recruited upon graduation.

(B) And how was the result?

(C) They moved to another company before coming to us.

24. **Where do you want to go for your winter vacation, Pamela?**

(A) I love to go to Switzerland for skiing.

(B) My vacation is quite long.

(C) It's too cold in winter.

25. **Are you happy with your transfer to the new department?**

(A) Absolutely, I am so happy.

(B) Yes, I can transfer to the new one.

(C) I am not moving to other company.

26. **Why don't we take a ten minute break before the next performance?**

(A) Yes, I've love to take it.

(B) I can say it is possible for the braking system.

(C) I think we can break it.

27. **Do you have a reservation for the Nelson Hotel?**

(A) I am still thinking about going.

(B) Yes, on Dec. 12th, confirmed.

(C) The place must be busy.

28. **When do you think you can you fill out this survey?**

(A) I'd be glad to.

(B) I'll file them this afternoon.

(C) It will take in about 10 minutes.

29. **Can you go out with me for the new movie?**

(A) Sure, why don't we meet at 7:00?

(B) It was more entertaining than the first movie.

(C) My father saw the movie.

30. **The new gadgetry will cost me an arm and a leg.**

(A) I'll send you my cost.

(B) I know, it is too expensive.

(C) The final cost is not fixed yet.

Chapter 8 Reading

Dialogue Challenge 8

Janet : Hello, Karl. I heard that you are a nerd. You dig a book and love to read.
What types of books do you like to read?

Karl : In fact, I read many books regardless of genres, but I am fond of reading fantasy and SF books. Nowadays, I read more books of Science Fiction.

Janet : Ha, ha, right. SF, or Science Fiction books are our contemporary these days. For me fantasy is my favorite.

Karl : Do you like to read Harry Potter series? I already read it, it was one of the most gripping, interesting, fascinating novel I've ever read in my life. And I know it's fiction and it's an imaginary world of fantasy. But the books gave me much energy, and fresh ideas influencing on the new designs of my career.

Janet : You are right. Some good books offer you a variety of ideas on your work and life, sometimes giving us an escape of the hard reality. In this harsh world we need some fantasies when we live our lives. Those books work as a kind of ventilation from the stuffy and suffocating reality.

Karl : Yeah, we can go through the hardships of life with the lessons and teaching from the good books. The beneficial books are something like our mentors and gurus in our lives.

Janet : But, alas, my poor eyesight is the only problem with reading books. I take a pill which is good for the eyesight every day. But I don't think it is good for my eyes. Whenever I read a book, I am suffering from the dryness of them.

Karl : In that case, why don't you see an oculist before the deterioration of your eye sight? There is a famous eye doctor who is a graduate form the Harvard Medical School in the downtown.

Janet : I already saw him two times last month. He insisted me to have an eye surgery. So I am scared of it.

Karl : I am sorry to hear that. It is really hard to keep your body healthy in this busy world. We come to ruin our body while catching up with the speedy and harsh reality.

Sentence Challenge 8

01. I read many books regardless of genres.

02. I am fond of reading fantasy and SF books.

03. It was one of the most gripping, interesting, fascinating novel I've ever read in my life.

04. The books gave me much energy, and fresh ideas influencing on the new designs of my career.

05. Some good books offer you a variety of ideas on your work and life.

06. Those books work as a kind of ventilation from the stuffy and suffocating reality.

07. We can go through the hardships of life with the lessons and teaching from the good books.

08. The beneficial books are something like our mentors and gurus in our lives.

09. My poor eyesight is the only problem with reading books.

10. I take a pill which is good for the eyesight every day.

11. Whenever I read a book, I am suffering from the dryness of them.

12. Why don't you see an oculist before the deterioration of your eye sight?

13. It is really hard to keep your body healthy in this busy world.

14. We come to ruin our body while catching up with the speedy and harsh reality.

Grammar Challenge 8

It occurred to me that (subject + verb)

The word 'occurred' tells somebody that something has come to mind or has been found. You allow them to know that you come to have the thought on something.

Here are some examples:

"It occurred to me that I should do my homework."
"It occurred to me that we should work out on a regular basis."
"It occurred to me that we should donate our fortune before we die."
"It occurred to me that we live in the busy world."
"It occurred to me that babies are vulnerable to any diseases."

When we use 'had' or 'has' in front of 'occurred to', it delivers the feeling and intend of past memory and thought.

Here are some examples:

"It had occurred to me that my father already left home."
"It had occurred to me that I might see an oculist."
"It has occurred to me that I should celebrate my friend's birthday."
"It has occurred to me that she would tell me the truth."

Paragraph Challenge 8

Questions 1–4 refer to the following paragraph.

As you know, the number of population in L.A. has risen 1.________ over 5 years. Due to the increased number of 2.________ in the city, we have faced the problems of costly living cost and inflation of prices surrounding communities. Also the cost of available local housing is 3.______ the rise. Insufficient living condition results in more increased matters of the homeless. It 4.________ to me that the municipal authorities will take care of those problems for the well being of the citizens.

01. (A) climb
(B) significantly
(C) significant
(D) climbing

02. (A) residing
(B) reside
(C) residential
(D) residents

03. (A) to
(B) beyond
(C) to
(D) on

04. (A) occurred
(B) expended
(C) approached
(D) experimented

Conversation Challenge 8

01. Who told you about your company's M&A?

(A) I told him that he is in charge of it.

(B) You're a M&A merchant.

(C) It was announced in yesterday's boarding meeting.

02. How far is Dalevill from here, Mr. Molton?

(A) I don't know. but it is quite a long distance.

(B) John lives in Dalevill.

(C) We're going there tomorrow.

03. Why don't you tell Mr. Johnson for your pay raise?

(A) I'm afraid he will refuse it.

(B) Of course I'll help my friend.

(C) No, they didn't tell me the truth.

04. **Can you tell me the exact way to Maxim street?**

(A) It is 100 percent increase from my offer.
(B) You should take the route No. 2 from here.
(C) You should have your own Maxim.

05. **How much is the cost to have our old house remodeled?**

(A) The estimate is 10,000 dollars.
(B) By next day, they will set to remodel the house.
(C) The living room is remodeled.

06. **Can you tell me when the courier service will come?**

(A) I'll let you know what is it.
(B) I think the service will not come to us, today.
(C) You delivered a package for us.

07. **I don't know where is the rest room for men.**

(A) She's in the rest room.
(B) I'm new here, too. Please ask a janitor over there.
(C) I am not going to the rest room.

08. **Can you tell me where the office of chairman?**

(A) This is the chairman.

(B) The chairman's name is John Walker.

(C) It's on the top floor of the building.

09. **How much do you want to have your hair cut?**

(A) I'd like to use a shortcut.

(B) As short as it is.

(C) I go to a salon every day.

10. **Do you like to watch SF movies, Janet?**

(A) Yes, they taste sweet.

(B) No, I am a big fan of San Francisco.

(C) That's my favorite type of movies.

11. **When does the boss want the report to be done?**

(A) I thought the boss went out with it.

(B) It is due next week.

(C) Leave it on the boss' desk.

12. **Do you subscribe a Messenger Daily online?**

(A) Yes, every day by my mobile phone.

(B) Every weekend is good for me.

(C) Yes, she does.

13. **Why do you buy the apartment? You are leaving here.**

(A) No, I like to buy it now.

(B) For the investment

(C) I haven't decided it yet.

14. **Weren't you supposed to walk your dog every day?**

(A) I think it's okay to walk the dog.

(B) I got up late with the news.

(C) I couldn't. I was sick today.

15. **Who will be the mechanic to take care of the oil change for the car?**

(A) I think Mr. Conrad is a professional.

(B) I chose Mr. Parkerson for it.

(C) Taking care of it is hard for me.

16. **Do you stress the importance of being on time to your employees?**

(A) Yes, It is very important.

(B) At 9 A.M., I guess.

(C) No, I don't think it is well done.

17. **How can we get to the place of Mr. Dickerson's birthday party?**

(A) We can take a bus from the exit 9 from the gate of the metro station.

(B) It's not too far.

(C) I want to see him someday.

18. **Shall I take you more papers and ink from the storage room?**

(A) This printer is out of ink.

(B) The extra paper is in the storage room.

(C) Yes, you should. Thank you for your help.

19. **How are you presenting your newly released car today?**

(A) It is going well and I am happy.

(B) I want it presented in the show.

(C) I'd like to, but I can't release it.

20. **Would you mind recommending Mr. Johnson as CEO of our company?**

(A) It's too late.

(B) No, he is the perfect for the position.

(C) That's quite expensive, as far as I know.

21. **Can you tell me when the speaker will come for the seminar?**

(A) She will be here in half an hour.

(B) No, I don't think he really speaks.

(C) Actually, he seemed to speak well.

22. **Don't you have your insurance renewed?**

(A) Yes, I mailed the insurance for you.

(B) I've already have it extended.

(C) Yes, I'm happy with the insurance.

23. **Do you remember to make a reservation for the air line?**

(A) Of course. It has already been confirmed on December 24th.

(B) There are too many air lines.

(C) Yes, everyone got a reservation.

24. **I heard Mr. Parkerson got promoted last month.**

(A) Since he was born

(B) Congratulations!

(C) Who told you?

25. **Is the new employee in the department of accounting?**

(A) That's right, he is a novice now.

(B) He just walks in the morning.

(C) Yes, the department is dealing with the accounting.

26. **What are the requirements to apply for the company?**

(A) Gilbert is a very hard worker.

(B) At least five year's experience in the accounting

(C) You could probably work for the day shift.

27. **Who will participate in the negotiation with the Chinese company?**

(A) In the large meeting room.

(B) They negotiated the whole morning.

(C) Mr. Karltopher will do it.

28. **Would you like to go to the movies tonight with me?**

(A) I have to go with you, since I love to.

(B) I am a little bit late.

(C) It comes to 100 dollars.

29. **Do you know why Mrs. Susie is late tonight?**

(A) Well, I hear so.

(B) Yes, she does.

(C) She's called in sick ten minutes ago.

30. **Are you going to sign up for the class next semester?**

(A) Be careful, the sign board can fall anytime.

(B) Yes, I am. I heard the professor is the top authorities in the chemistry.

(C) We have the autographs of the celebrities.

Chapter 9 Food

Dialogue Challenge 9

Janet : Good evening, Karl. What are you doing here? Do you want to buy some sweet stuffs?

Karl : Hi, Janet. I came here to take a look at the newly released chocolate boxes as the christmas present for my son. My son has a sweet tooth, he really loves to eat chocolate bars.

Janet : I heard Belgian chocolate is the most famous and tasty. But regardless of the producing countries, you see we enjoy chocolate everywhere, whatever occasion we have for celebration. My daughter likes to eat chocolate, too.

Karl : Children really love to have chocolate. As you know, this shop has the specialty of Belgian truffles. My son likes to have chocolate truffles.

Janet : Well, your son is the real chocolate lover. But I am afraid your son will be suffering from the cavities due to the excessive consumption of chocolate.

Karl : He already got some cavities. He got the experience of replacing his teeth.

His molar has been changed with the artificial dent.

Janet : We should be careful with eating chocolate too. It also has much caffeine.

Karl : You are right. But I have no choice but to eat chocolate. Chocolate gives me much energy when I am tired. The sweet ingredients of it releases our fatigue.

My favorite type is the Brussel Sprouts. The taste of it is fantastic. Have you ever tried the Brussel Sprouts? Oh, God, it is helpless when you taste it. It is melting instantly when you have it in your mouth. I know we should have a healthy diet.

But sometimes your intake of chocolate can be helpful when we are exhausted.

Janet : Yeah, you are right. Taking some sweets like chocolate and candies can give us energy when we consume too much of calories. But we should not take excessive amount of the sweets. We will suffer from dental diseases, obesity, and diabetes.

Karl : You're right. We should concede that too much is as bad as too little.

Sentence Challenge 9

01. I came here to take a look at the newly released chocolate boxes as the christmas present for my son.

02. I heard Belgian chocolate is the most famous and tasty.

03. But regardless of the producing countries, you see we enjoy chocolate everywhere, whatever occasion we have for celebration.

04. As you know, this shop has the specialty of Belgian truffles.

05. I am afraid your son will be suffering from the cavities due to the excessive consumption of chocolate.

06. His molar has been changed with the artificial dent.

07. I have no choice but to eat chocolate.

08. The sweet ingredients of it releases our fatigue.

09. It is helpless when you taste it.

10. It is melting instantly when you have it in your mouth.

11. Sometimes your intake of chocolate can be helpful when we are exhausted.

12. Taking some sweets like chocolate and candies can give us energy when we consume too much of calories.

13. We should not take excessive amount of the sweets.

14. We will suffer from dental diseases, obesity, and diabetes.

15. We should concede that too much is as bad as too little.

Grammar Challenge 9

You'd better + (verb)

The expression of 'You'd' is a contraction of 'you had' or 'you would.' You are inducing and suggesting a certain kind of action for people.

Here are some examples:

"You'd better go to bed."
"You'd better take a nap."
"You'd better have a break."
"You'd better go right now."
"You'd better leave me alone."
"You'd better come to the class early."
"You'd better work hard for your future."
"You'd better study English hard."
"You'd better trust me regardless of the situation."
"You'd better go on a diet."

Paragraph Challenge 9

Questions 1–4 refer to the following paragraph.

For the coffee lovers a doctor says that you have no problems when you drink as 1.______ as you want. The doctor is professor, Durex, who is one of the authorities on coffee, a director of the Institute for Coffee Studies at New York University. He's even 2.________ a metric for monitoring your dosage. But the doctor recommends that you should 3.______ back on the consumption of coffee only when you can't sleep at night. If you don't have any problems with your sleep at night, he advises that you can drink to the amount you like. He also insists that it's not going to do you any 4.______, and it will actually help you.

01. (A) much
(B) lighter
(C) many
(D) lot

02. (A) added
(B) imitated
(C) developed
(D) said

03. (A) drink
(B) increase
(C) cut
(D) drop

04. (A) harmed
(B) harms
(C) harm
(D) harmful

Conversation Challenge 9

01. **Where Mr. Parkerson is going for his business trip?**

(A) I have a meeting at 12:00.
(B) You want to go to lunch with them?
(C) He is planning to leave for L.A.

02. **When do you want my report to be submitted?**

(A) About 10 reports
(B) It should be reported.
(C) No later than next Tuesday

03. **Why did they postpone the board meeting?**

(A) Yes, I met them.
(B) Because something urgent happened.
(C) It was a real surprise.

04. **What was your job when you worked for Tompson Inc.?**

(A) I went to Tompson last month.

(B) I worked as an accountant.

(C) Business is not easy at all.

05. **Have you ever accomplished your dream of being a lawyer?**

(A) No, I can't even imaginc it.

(B) Absolutely, I already became a partner at the law firm.

(C) The whole dreamer was too foolish.

06. **How do you make this sofa so comfortable?**

(A) We use the expensive and effective latex for it.

(B) No thank you. I've had made it.

(C) I guess it's not easy.

07. **Do we have to buy the new printer today or tomorrow?**

(A) We don't have to, it has already arrived.

(B) The order is not canceled.

(C) For the news printing system

08. **How much will it cost to have a new refrigerator?**

(A) By December 11th
(B) I had it checked already.
(C) About over two million dollars

09. **When did the mechanic say he would come to the office?**

(A) It's under 100 kilometers.
(B) At around 4:00
(C) If you come to the office, we will appreciate it.

10. **When did you get this project done?**

(A) When you ordered me to do it.
(B) Lots of projects are left.
(C) Let's go over the profect.

11. **Do you want the department of human resources to hire more?**

(A) Whenever it is possible, we need more people.
(B) And how many people are in there?
(C) Neither do I.

12. **Who is in charge of taking care of the accounting figures?**

(A) Tompson took the report to look into the figures.
(B) I have an exact figure
(C) Our new comer at the department of budgeting

13. **Did you have a file for the backup?**

(A) Yes, just for the future use
(B) My back is killing me.
(C) We go back to check the file.

14. **Will you forward your e-mail to the boss, today?**

(A) Nobody e-mail me.
(B) Don't worry. I already did the job.
(C) Thank you so much.

15. **What happened to the banks today?**

(A) They are all closed because of holidays.
(B) Yes, it's the new holiday.
(C) No, problem.

16. **Would you like to work as a full-timer for the company?**

(A) That makes sense.

(B) Absolutely, I want to.

(C) That's not important for the boss.

17. **What is the address of our supplier for the main boards?**

(A) It's 522 at Kensington Street.

(B) The supplier is not here.

(C) I think it's the important board.

18. **How about mending your presentation script before it starts.**

(A) No, I don't know the presentation.

(B) Actually, I already did.

(C) Mind your manner.

19. **Do you have any pills for a toothache?**

(A) I have my tooth pulled out.

(B) Yes, I have a painkiller now.

(C) That's the worst.

20. **How about accepting the new offer?**

(A) I didn't say a word.

(B) We offer a 50 percent discount.

(C) Well, I will just stay at this company.

21. **How often do I have to check the e-mails for the company?**

(A) I wash my car checked yet.

(B) Twice a day before you leave the office.

(C) I'll e-mail you right now.

22. **Do you like to use your smart watch?**

(A) Here's my watch.

(B) No, it is not short.

(C) Yes, it is very convenient.

23. **I heard you earned enormous amount of money.**

(A) Yes, I was so lucky.

(B) I put it back in my wallet.

(C) They made a lot of efforts.

24. **When do you want to go on a picnic for us?**

(A) We are going to go on a picnic to the beach.

(B) Anytime will be fine.

(C) Probably we are moving the furniture.

25. **Are you going to go to celebrate the boss's birthday?**

(A) Yes, I am inviting the boss.

(B) No, I am leaving for New York.

(C) I like the boss.

26. **Will you join us for playing chess, Dave?**

(A) Why are you late?

(B) Yes, it is my favorite.

(C) I am late, too.

27. **Do you think I should send this parcel before the Christmas Day?**

(A) Sure, you are in charge of it.

(B) There's a mailbox for him.

(C) I bought a Christmas parcel yesterday.

28. **Could you tell me about the cause of your success?**

(A) Yes, I could tell you that I worked almost 16 hours a day.

(B) Sure, what do you want to hear?

(C) Today is a very successful day.

29. **How did you make the sales figures?**

(A) I figured them out now.

(B) Sales dramatically plummeted last month.

(C) It was based on the data you gave to me.

30. **I'm planning to buy you a new smart phone.**

(A) Yes, the new smart phone is good.

(B) You are not smart guy.

(C) Wow, I am really happy with the news.

Chapter 10 Dining

Dialogue Challenge 10

Janet : Now Karl, we had the wonderful steak at the Italian bistro. Thank you for your treat and kindness.

Karl : Well, the Italian restaurant carries a variety of fresh organic vegetables fruits, vegetables, meat, and wines. It is not that cheap, but it deserves the price.

Janet : Yeah, I really like to eat the delicacies of all the seasons.

Karl : Well when it comes to delicacy, the restaurant is second to none serving the delicious food in the region. The restaurant has the philosophy of food and gastronomy.

Janet : Gastronomy is quite an academic word, which is the study of preparing and serving delicate and appetizing foods, and the science of good eating. Additionally gastronomists are scientists who deal with the study of gastronomy.

Most of the gastronomists are interested in various recipes and making exotic foods. More over practical gastronomy is related with the practice and study of the preparation, production, and service of the various foods around the world.

Karl : Wow, you must be a doctor of foods. How did you know the theoretical aspects of foods? Are you interested in the field of foods?

Janet : Yest, I wanted to be a renowned chef, but I changed my mind to study food science. The field is quite intriguing to me. As you know, there is the new study of genetical food. That is to say, genetically modified foods or GM foods.

Most GM foods come from cash crops in high demand by farmers such as soybean, corn, canola, and cotton. There is a scientific consensus that currently available foods derived from GM crops affect no greater harm to human health than conventional foods. But each GM food needs to be tested on a case-by-case basis before its serving to human.

Karl : Unbelievable, you should be a professor at the department of Food Science or Food Engineering. Your story is quite informative. I can get much benefit when I have a talk with you.

Janet : Well, thank you for your compliment.

Sentence Challenge 10

01. Thank you for your treat and kindness.

02. The Italian restaurant carries a variety of fresh organic vegetables fruits, vegetables, meat, and wines.

03. I really like to eat the delicacies of all the seasons.

04. l when it comes to delicacy, the restaurant is second to none serving the delicious food in the region.

05. The restaurant has the philosophy of food and gastronomy.

06. Gastronomy is quite an academic word, which is the study of preparing and serving delicate and appetizing foods, and the science of good eating.

07. Gastronomists are scientists who deal with the study of gastronomy.

08. More over practical gastronomy is related with the practice and study of the preparation, production, and service of the various foods around the world.

09. How did you know the theoretical aspects of foods? Are you interested in the field of foods?

10. The field is quite intriguing to me.

11. Most GM foods come from cash crops in high demand by farmers such as soybean, corn, canola, and cotton.

12. There is a scientific consensus that currently available foods derived from GM crops affect no greater harm to human health than conventional foods.

13. Your story is quite informative.

Grammar Challenge 10

It's no use + (verb-ing)

'It's' is a contraction for 'it is.' When you say 'It's' no use', you are telling what someone is doing is useless and unrecommendable.

Here are some examples:

"It's no use telling a lie."

"It's no use giving your son pocket money."

"It's no use seeing a doctor late."

"It's no use fighting with here."

"It's no use quarreling with your wife."

"It's no use staying at night."

"It's no use telling me the truth."

"It's no use leaving her alone."

"It's no use vacuuming the room."

"It's no use cleaning the desk."

Paragraph Challenge 10

Questions 1–4 refer to the following paragraph.

Your intent of taking a vacation is a good 1._______. Travelling for recreation is sometimes a luxury that only wealthy people can 2._______. But nowadays, many people in the world are enjoying travelling by means of 3._______ a vacation. Regardless of their income and wealth, people are happy when they are taking a break from work. But, as you know, it is 4._________ that you should take the permission from your supervisor before your leave when you are employed.

01. (A) idea
(B) day
(C) ideas
(D) days

02. (A) affording
(B) affords
(C) affordable
(D) afford

03. (A) takes
(B) taking
(C) taken
(D) take

04. (A) wish
(B) required
(C) requires
(D) wishes

Conversation Challenge 10

01. **Mrs. Callaway, where do you want to go with Mr. Markerson for lunch?**

(A) At 10:00

(B) No, he is not here.

(C) To an Indian diner

02. **When are you going to leave for L.A.?**

(A) No, it's too late.

(B) In two days

(C) I should go to L.A.

03. **If you are not busy, would you show me how to use the copier?**

(A) Yes, here is the copier.

(B) No, I don't want you to use it.

(C) Sure, wait a moment

04. **The milk in the refrigerator doesn't look good to drink.**

(A) It's gone, be careful not to have it.

(B) He doesn't eat milk.

(C) No, I didn't drink milk.

05. **What's the agenda for today's board meeting?**

(A) You should know that it has been canceled.

(B) Yes, the agenda is important.

(C) They will board the train.

06. **How many applicants apply for the company?**

(A) More than 200.

(B) As much as I can.

(C) I applied for it yesterday.

07. **Do we have to fix the camera, today?**

(A) Because I am not taking the photos.

(B) No, it is not that urgent.

(C) Yes, the camera is expensive.

08. **Who will pick up the package in the lobby?**

(A) No, the package is expensive to be delivered.

(B) Let me take care of it, while I am going there.

(C) The lobby is always busy.

09. **What do you want for your birthday present?**

(A) Because the present boss is a smart leader.

(B) A piece of new glasses

(C) Yes, it is my birthday.

10. **What are you planning to do for your summer leave?**

(A) I will travel Italy this time.

(B) I have to fly over to L.A.

(C) Yes, planning is important.

11. **How can I get to the Melvil Hotel?**

(A) Yes, you should be able to.

(B) You'd better take the bus No. 110 at the bus stop.

(C) No, I want to walk alone.

12. **What do you do for your living?**

(A) I put it in the living room.

(B) No, they will live up to 100.

(C) I am a sales man.

13. **How are you doing these days, Mrs. Pamela?**

(A) I am quite good.

(B) No, I'll do it right now.

(C) I am so young to go to school.

14. **When are you going to see your professor?**

(A) At the living room

(B) No, the professor is not here.

(C) He wants to have a meeting with me at 10:00.

15. **Who is your boss to make the final decision on the project?**

(A) The man sitting on the chair in the office.

(B) Yes, it it final.

(C) No, I don't like the project.

16. **Is Mr. Johnson your successor, Amelia?**

(A) Yes, he's a nice guy.

(B) He is in charge of our company.

(C) I think so.

17. **When are you going to have the presentation?**

(A) Yes, I have to present it.

(B) We need our presentation.

(C) Maybe next Friday

18. **How long will it take to get to the airport from here?**

(A) More than an hour

(B) I wasn't ready to go to the airport.

(C) The airport is very huge.

19. **When is your apartment's house warming party?**

(A) Next Monday evening

(B) The apartment is not large enough.

(C) He wants me to go to the apartment.

20. **Who is in charge of dealing with the contract?**

(A) I should be in charge of the bill.
(B) My boss is handling it.
(C) No, I don't know the contract.

21. **The refrigerator is out of order now, what should I do?**

(A) Yes, the fridge is the ordered one.
(B) I like to buy the refrigerator.
(C) Just call the department of customer service to take care of it.

22. **Is Johnson & Johnson Inc. located near here?**

(A) Yes, it is just next to our building
(B) I will locate the lost item.
(C) We are not satisfied with it.

23. **How about the sales figure of this month?**

(A) It is quite good, but the boss is not satisfied with it.
(B) We can figure it out.
(C) We have no sales team.

24. **How do you get to your workplace?**

(A) The place is closed today.

(b) The workplace is really far away from his home.

(C) I go to work on foot every day.

25. **Is the company a spinoff from the conglomerate?**

(A) Not at all, it is a big company itself.

(B) No, I can take it off.

(C) The company is far away off the main street.

26. **Excuse me, can you tell me the way to operate the new software?**

(A) Mind your own business.

(B) I don't think it is the right software.

(C) Sure thing, I will be right back to you.

27. **Is the insurance covering all the expenses of a car accident?**

(A) Yes, they are covering us.

(B) Definitely, every cost of it.

(C) No, it is his insurance.

28. **Thank you for the wonderful dinner, Mr. Wood.**

(A) You're welcome. I am happy with your content.

(B) No, it's not a dinner but a lunch.

(C) Yes, it is expensive one.

29. **Do you expect your second baby, Mrs. Kerry?**

(A) Yes, my baby is the top priority.

(B) Yes, he is the second to none.

(C) Yes, I am happy with the truth.

30. **Why don't you hand the paperwork to the assistant, Marry?**

(A) I should take care of it myself, I think.

(B) There are many assistants.

(C) Yes, you can give me a hand.

Answers

Chapter 1. Teaching

Paragraph Challenge 1

Questions 1-4 refer to the following paragraph.

Ten years ago, Mrs. Kimberly signed a three-year rent to open her fancy restaurant, Kimberly Cuisine, at Kensington Avenue. Mrs. Kimberly were happy with many 1._______ these days. "Our dishes are based on fresh and organic ingredients" she was very proud of the fact. But actually Mrs. Kimberly 2. _______ from the low profit at the beginning stage. Nowadays, the restaurant is very 3._______ and became a famous place in the region. Additionally she is planning to open 4._______ branch at Plum Avenue.

01. (A) person
(B) porters
(C) customers
(D) waiters

Answer **(c)**

02. (A) suffered
(B) frustrated
(C) pleased
(D) booked

Answer (a)

03. (A) crowd
(B) crowded
(C) crowds
(D) crowding

Answer (b)

04. (A) other
(B) another
(C) others
(D) anothers

Answer (b)

Conversation Challenge 1

01. **Where's your company located?**

(A) On Pine Street

(B) No, it wasn't expensive.

(C) Location is convenient.

Answer (a)

02. **When is the end of the today's conference?**

(A) At the News stand

(B) Conference is important.

(C) Around 12 o'clock

Answer (c)

03. **Where is the annual ceremony held?**

(A) Yes, it was across here.

(B) I know it is true.

(C) At the auditorium.

Answer (c)

04. **Who's the CEO of your company next year?**

(A) In this town
(B) The stage
(C) Mrs. Watson

Answer (c)

05. **Where do you think the orientation for the new comers will be held?**

(A) Starting next year
(B) In this conference room
(C) For the comers

Answer (b)

06. **Have you ever met with your new client?**

(A) Yes, I already met her.
(B) No, they didn't.
(C) That's a new project.

Answer (a)

07. **Are you going to go to the movies this weekend?**

(A) I've gone to the movies.
(B) A new seasonal movie
(C) Sure, I and Jennifer will go there.

Answer (c)

08. **Is the department store near here?**

(A) It stores 100 giga bites.

(B) It's an expensive department store.

(C) Yes, it is 1 mile away.

Answer (c)

09. **Where should I put the parcel, ma'am?**

(A) Right over there.

(B) By next morning

(C) Mr. Parkerson will take care of the parcel.

Answer (a)

10. **Can you please show me how to turn on the air conditioner?**

(A) Yes, I can help you.

(B) It's already ten o'clock.

(C) Please show me the way.

Answer (a)

11. **Would you give me a hand to make some copies of the report?**

(A) Yes, I can. anytime call me.

(B) It makes good copies.

(C) Yes, for ten years.

Answer (a)

12. **Where did you get the management consulting?**

(A) I'll have nowhere.

(B) From the Mckinge Company.

(C) Two hours of consulting

Answer (b)

13. **Who is the new applicant for the company?**

(A) I think Mrs. Pamela.

(B) Several applicants

(C) I plan to give the new resume.

Answer (a)

14. **How many times a day do the express trains stop here?**

(A) 10 dollars

(B) Turn to the left.

(C) At least 25.

Answer (c)

15. **How can I find the way to fix may broken notebook computer?**

(A) You'd better consult the repair and maintenance department.

(B) That's what I am saying.

(C) Try the computer.

Answer (a)

16. **Shall we buy more papers for the printer?**

(A) No, they're enough now.
(B) Yes, we're quite busy.
(C) Papers are expensive.

Answer (a)

17. **The company is going to be out of business at the end of the year.**

(A) Yes, I am sorry to hear that.
(B) The business is not ready yet.
(C) Do you know the company's CEO?

Answer (a)

18. **When does the performance of the idol group begin?**

(A) At around 7:00 p.m.
(B) He performs well.
(C) The group is large.

Answer (a)

19. **I'd like to have a newly ordered refrigerator in the kitchen.**

(A) She is in the kitchen.
(B) You can have new one this afternoon.
(C) A collection of refrigerators

Answer (b)

20. **We should change the date of our board meeting next week.**

(A) The board of directors will not come today.
(B) Okay, when do you want?
(C) About 100 people at the meeting

Answer (b)

21. **Why was the annual ceremony postponed?**

(A) I'll postpone the ceremony.
(B) The CEO is in the hospital.
(C) The ceremony is enormous.

Answer (b)

22. **How can I get to the museum of the arts?**

(A) You'd better take a taxi. It is quite a far way.
(B) Sure, I'll go to the museum.
(C) Only for 20 days.

Answer (a)

23. **We should finish this project by tomorrow.**

(A) Don't worry. Let me help you.
(B) On Pine Street.
(C) Let's find another project.

Answer (a)

24. **Was Mr. Karlbertson at the seminar yesterday?**

(A) It was informative.

(B) Yes, he attended there.

(C) From the seminary

Answer (b)

25. **Is it cheaper to buy the TV set on the internet?**

(A) Two million dollars

(B) It is quite a good quality.

(C) Much lower than the stores

Answer (c)

26. **Why wasn't Mr. Parker able to attend the meeting?**

(A) From the meeting.

(B) He is out of town for his business trip.

(C) Sometime next week.

Answer (b)

27. **Can't you find the way to boost the sales of the goods?**

(A) I think the goods have good quality.

(B) I did, but the market is very hostile.

(C) We all had good sales.

Answer (b)

28. **How many people are working on the new subsidiary?**

(A) About 300

(B) There's a new company.

(C) We work hard.

Answer (a)

29. **Can I have a feed on this new project.**

(A) Feed a new cat.

(B) Please check your email, I already sent it.

(C) Let's have a new project.

Answer (b)

30. **Who will help to move the boxes on the desk of Mr. Karlson?**

(A) Don't worry. we already did the job.

(B) He is not ready.

(C) A couple of hours ago.

Answer (a)

Chapter 2. How about the company?

Paragraph Challenge 2

Questions 1–4 refer to the following paragraph.

Thank you for your purchase of the Bright Washer. Many people are making an excellent 1.______. With a little amount of the Bright Washer, you can wash a lot of clothing clean and effectively at a time. You can have a 2.______ to save your precious money when you purchase the Bright Washer by bundles. The cleanness of the dirty clothes was already proved after 3.________washed by the Bright Washer. So, don't 4._____the chance of purchasing the Bright Washer. It is on sale now!

01. (A) chose
(B) choosing
(C) choosers
(D) choice

Answer (d)

02. (A) chance
(B) challenge
(C) change
(D) check

Answer (a)

03. (A) being
(B) proof
(C) was
(D) problem

Answer (a)

04. (A) loose
(B) lose
(C) lost
(D) loosen

Answer (b)

Conversation Challenge 2

01. **How would you like your coffee, Mr. Smith?**

(A) Yes, I'd like to know more.

(B) I don't know how.

(C) Cream and sugar please.

Answer **(c)**

02. **Have you heard the news from CNN this morning?**

(A) No, it's old.

(B) You mean about Jason Parker?

(C) I heard about that.

Answer **(b)**

03. **How about going out for lunch the weather outside is beautiful?**

(A) Yes, it sounds good.

(B) Yes, but I'll have to meet you there.

(C) No, thank you. I'm suffering from a diarrhea.

Answer **(c)**

04. **Josh, do you know when our next payment is due?**

(A) It should be here any minute now.
(B) As far as I know, 10th of every month.
(C) I'll pay for it this time.

Answer (b)

05. **Wow, you look handsome where did you get your haircut?**

(A) From the Marshall Salon.
(B) Yes, I did. Do you like it?
(C) I'm sorry. We don't like hairy products.

Answer (a)

06. **I am sorry to ask you would like to call me back after school?**

(A) Yes, but your school picture is great.
(B) Sure, I will reach you later.
(C) In about 20 minutes, but first I'll have to change the film.

Answer (b)

07. **Where do I speak to about getting a new cartridge?**

(A) Complete a capital equipment request form and submit it to Purchasing.
(B) I haven't asked the woman yet.
(C) I think they're using their cars.

Answer (a)

08. **Is that man in the lobby your customer, Johnson?**

(A) Yes, he is very important person for our company.

(B) No, I've never been there before.

(C) No, but there is a similarity

Answer (a)

09. **When are you going to take a vacation, Karl?**

(A) Yes, but I won't take it until next spring.

(B) Oh, really? When will you get back?

(C) Next month, maybe

Answer (c)

10. **Can you finish up by the end of the month, Mr. Tellerson?**

(A) Yes, that should give me plenty of time.

(B) I was planning to do some shopping this weekend.

(C) Yes, I believe I can.

Answer (c)

11. **Do you know that today is 30th anniversary of our company?**

(A) No, I guess I should get him a card or something.

(B) Yeah, I heard it last night.

(C) I'm not sure. I think he said it was in September.

Answer (b)

12. **Can you tell me what time the movie, Beauty and the Beast plays?**

(A) It's set in the tenth.

(B) It's only about 10 hours from here.

(C) A quarter to ten, I believe.

Answer (c)

13. **Do we need to purchase more petroleum for the heater?**

(A) No, we have enough for another month.

(B) Yes, we'd better be prepared for the cold winter.

(C) Yes, I'd like a little more, please.

Answer (b)

14. **How far is the Incheon train station from here?**

(A) It's only two blocks down, go past the Union bank.

(B) It doesn't stop now.

(C) We need more training sessions for the employees.

Answer (a)

15. **How was your first blind date with a lady?**

(A) About an hour.

(B) I am feeling quite well with her.

(C) No, I don't think we have. It's nice to meet you.

Answer (b)

16. **Is it still snowing outside, David?**

(A) No, I've finished.

(B) Yes, be careful with falling on the icy streets.

(C) No, I think it stopped.

Answer (b)

17. **Can I help your googling, boss?**

(A) No, thank you. I can handle it.

(B) You should turn it in to the lost and found.

(C) No, thanks. I'm just browsing

Answer (a)

18. **Would you sign up this contract with Marker and Spencer, please?**

(A) Where do I sign? Here?

(B) Yes, I think that's a good sign.

(C) No, I wouldn't. I should check more conditions.

Answer (c)

19. **How's the new employee's work performance?**

(A) I try to get as much exercise as I can.

(B) She sings well on the stage.

(C) Actually, he is a great asset for us.

Answer (c)

20. **Who's handling the new project, Mrs. Culberson?**

(A) Because of the holiday, we'll get paid a day early.

(B) The round ones do much better.

(C) Amie Jackson in the accounting department.

Answer (c)

21. **Would you get me some more papers while you going out now?**

(A) I'll leave in about ten minutes.

(B) Sure, how much do you need?

(C) I'll probably take my car.

Answer (b)

22. **Mr. President, what should I tell Mr. Johnson when he calls?**

(A) Oh, really? What did he say?

(B) Yes, you should.

(C) Tell him I am out of the town.

Answer (c)

23. **Would you please turn off your smart phone? We are at the concert.**

(A) Sure, what do you want to hear?

(B) Yes, I like this too.

(C) Oh, I'm sorry. I will do it right now.

Answer (c)

24. **When you are free, could you check this document, Mrs. Peggy?**

(A) No, there was nothing for you.

(B) I think it'll be here any minute.

(C) Sure, just give me two hours, sir.

Answer (c)

25. **When are you going to have your day off?**

(A) This Friday when it is possible.

(B) Yes, but I'll probably do some work at home anyway.

(C) I did, but I took some medicine that cleared it up.

Answer (a)

26. **How would you like your steak, sir?**

(A) That's a good price. I'll take the steak.

(B) Well done, please.

(C) Yes, I'll pay for it.

Answer (b)

27. **Is the accountant working right with those figures?**

(A) Yes, he is doing well, don't worry.

(B) When I last saw them they were on the left.

(C) O.K. I'll take what's left.

Answer (a)

28. **Do you want your lunch packed?**

(A) I'd like it to go, please.
(B) No, I am going to eat here.
(C) Sure, that's no problem.

Answer (b)

29. **Are you promising to give me a pay raise, sir?**

(A) No, I have no other appointments.
(B) Really? What did he say?
(C) Of course. You deserve it.

Answer (c)

30. **What time shall I come back here to meet the representative?**

(A) How abut noon, sir?
(B) Sure, tomorrow sounds fine.
(C) Maybe tomorrow will be late.

Answer (a)

Chapter 3. Social Network Service

Paragraph Challenge 3

Questions 1–4 refer to the following paragraph.

The Metropolitan Messenger is an independent community newspaper that has 1.______ for the residents of Boston for over 130 years. All of our articles are 2. ________ by the journalists employed by the Metropolitan Messenger. Copies of the Metropolitan Messenger are also 3.________ at the City Hall, Town Cafe, and almost every convenient store in the county. Any articles or photographs that are used in the newspapers reserve the copy rights. Especially articles from the Metropolitan Messenger will be available at the 4.________ of every week by papers and electronically.

01. (A) served
(B) participated
(C) called
(D) represented

Answer **(a)**

02. (A) writers
(B) wrote
(C) writing
(D) written

Answer (d)

03. (A) avail
(B) available
(C) avails
(D) availing

Answer (b)

04. (A) begin
(B) beginners
(C) begins
(D) beginning

Answer (d)

Conversation Challenge 3

01. **When will you release the marketable smart phone, Mr. Johnson?**

(A) At the office.
(B) This upcoming Thursday, I believe.
(C) The last time I saw you.

Answer (b)

02. **Do you know why my reserved air ticket has been canceled?**

(A) Because you mJanet a phone call of cancelation last week
(B) Yes, I can cancel it.
(C) It's not far from LA.

Answer (a)

03. **Where did you purchase the long goose jacket?**

(A) Only 10 bucks
(B) For Canada
(C) From the internet shopping mall.

Answer (c)

04. **We are running out of gas, is there any gas station near here?**

(A) Yes, it is located two blocks away from where we are.
(B) The station's very busy.
(C) I will run this evening for my health.

Answer (a)

05. **How many people attended the party?**

(A) At least 100 gallons.
(B) He's the party animal.
(C) It is countless.

Answer (c)

06. **Can you tell me the way to the Central station?**

(A) About 20 minutes.
(B) I need to go to the station.
(C) Take the bus number 511.

Answer (c)

07. **Where is an ATM in the precinct?**

(A) Anytime in the afternoon.
(B) No, ATM doesn't mean Automatic Trans Mission.
(C) In front of the department of accounting.

Answer (c)

08. **We are not supposed to use internet at work, why?**

(A) The maintenance staff.
(B) To prevent a thief
(C) That is the order of the boss.

Answer **(c)**

09. **When do you expect we can finish up the project?**

(A) The same finisher
(B) You are not expecting
(C) At least at the beginning of next month.

Answer **(c)**

10. **Will you give me a hand when I move the plant to the department of personnel?**

(A) I'd love to.
(B) Don't worry. I will not be there.
(C) Right when you are free.

Answer **(a)**

11. **Can you imagine that we are not going to get a pay raise?**

(A) A full-time service
(B) At the bottom of the ground
(C) Don't worry. the boss promised to increase our salary.

Answer **(c)**

12. **When can we get a maintenance service for the copier?**

(A) In about two hours
(B) I'm not maintain the department.
(C) Service is not good enough.

Answer (a)

13. **Your wife is expecting your baby next month, isn't she?**

(A) Right, how did you know that?
(B) I love a baby.
(C) Expectation is limited.

Answer (a)

14. **I'd like to make a reservation of air ticket for Boston.**

(A) Boston is far away from here.
(B) An airline is bankrupted.
(C) No, problem. Let me help you sir.

Answer (c)

15. **How do you get to work by car pool or by train?**

(A) We share a ride for the purpose of energy saving.
(B) That doesn't work very well.
(C) Train is not leaving now.

Answer (a)

16. **When will you make a presentation for the project?**

(A) Tomorrow, you should be attendant.

(B) The presentation will not be long.

(C) I can handle the project.

Answer (a)

17. **Our company is looking for an excellent designer of the outdoor fashion.**

(A) About 10 percent discount

(B) I heard that news.

(C) Didn't you have it designed?

Answer (b)

18. **Are you on Facebook when are you free?**

(A) I don't know it much.

(B) She posts a lot of photos on it.

(C) Yes, when I am not busy.

Answer (c)

19. **Please be careful not to catch a cold, it is frigid outside.**

(A) You can have a seat outside.

(B) Thank you, I hate the cold weather.

(C) OK, we will carefully deal with the frozen meat.

Answer (b)

20. **Who is the representative of the customer service satisfaction department?**

(A) Mr. John is in charge of it.

(B) They are not representing the company.

(C) I can be satisfied with it.

Answer (a)

21. **Do we have to post an opening at the classified ads right now?**

(A) I waited for the new comers.

(B) Maybe, we will hire him.

(C) No, it isn't necessary.

Answer (c)

22. **Where can I get the information concerning your article?**

(A) Another a couple of hours

(B) Call him right now.

(C) From my office

Answer (c)

23. **I have a medical checkup today, what should be watched out?**

(A) I'm a medical doctor.

(B) Don't drink even water.

(C) We watched him recently.

Answer (b)

24. **How much is the courier service?**

(A) It depends on the weight of package.
(B) I can serve you right now.
(C) No, it isn't not expensive.

Answer (a)

25. **Why do I have to clean up the sink at the lab?**

(A) Yes, I hope to use the lab.
(B) For the next person to use
(C) They're going to clean the lab.

Answer (b)

26. **How about the production line of the smart phones?**

(A) It is going well right now.
(B) The smart phones are expensive.
(C) A production line is located on the second floor.

Answer (a)

27. **Would you like another cup of coffee?**

(A) At the coffee shop
(B) I'd love to
(C) I will order right now.

Answer (b)

28. **Why don't you use the new software, Daven?**

(A) I can't afford it.

(B) It is not expensive.

(C) Every software is worth it.

Answer (a)

29. **When is the presentation for the new users of the released game?**

(A) I should present it.

(B) They'll need the new games.

(C) It has been postponed until next month.

Answer (c)

30. **Why were you late for joining our company?**

(A) Because I didn't finish up my graduate degree.

(B) I have another appointment.

(C) A few weeks later

Answer (a)

Chapter 4. Dream Jobs

Paragraph Challenge 4

Questions 1–4 refer to the following paragraph.

This is to let you know that during the Thanks giving holidays, we will be 1.________ discounted sales items in every Radio Shack store. For this event you should bring the coupons from the Daily Rivervill which is our weekly 2.________ in the county. During the holidays you can purchase the electronic goods 3.______ a remarkably cheap price. Please do not lose the big chance for 4.______ your money during the holiday season.

01. (A) offering
(B) have offering
(C) accepting
(D) accepted

Answer **(a)**

02. (A) newer
(B) books
(C) newspaper
(D) notebooks

Answer (c)

03. (A) at
(B) before
(C) beyond
(D) due

Answer (a)

04. (A) save
(B) saving
(C) saves
(D) saver

Answer (b)

Conversation Challenge 4

01. **How many people did attend the seminar at the University of Tulsa?**

(A) Let's meet at the university.

(B) It was a good seminar

(C) Almost 100 students

Answer **(c)**

02. **What kinds of kitchen stuffs does your company make?**

(A) Especially stoves

(B) The production line makes

(C) Yes, I like the kitchen work.

Answer **(a)**

03. **How can I order the food at this diner?**

(A) No thank you, I'll have some later.

(B) It's a new diner.

(C) Please, push the button on the table.

Answer **(c)**

04. How can I reach an ATM from here?

(A) Just walk to the student hall.

(B) Yes, I have an ATM

(C) That's a large ATM.

Answer (a)

05. When do you think I can see your boss?

(A) Maybe you are right.

(B) My boss is a good gentleman.

(C) Just after the lunch time

Answer (c)

06. Do you know who wants to have the fax machine fixed?

(A) I should have my fax.

(B) The boss of our company

(C) Thanks, that's a good idea.

Answer (b)

07. Do you prefer to leave the office now or later?

(A) It's quite preferable.

(B) I'm good now.

(C) I'd better leave in two hours.

Answer (c)

08. **Do you happen to know the route 110?**

(A) Across a small bridge.

(B) Sure, go straight, and turn right at the intersection.

(C) You could lower it a little bit.

Answer **(b)**

09. **How can I reach the lab in Johnson and Johnson?**

(A) It is not within my reach.

(B) An yearly leave will be fine.

(C) After getting a permission front desk, use the elevator.

Answer **(c)**

10. **Where can I find your company in the Jackson County?**

(A) Where is the counter?

(B) You can give me a call at the airport, and I will pick you up.

(C) Have you checked the my desk?

Answer **(b)**

11. **I am really happy to get a concert ticket of One Direction.**

(A) I am happy, too.

(B) One direction is sometimes dangerous.

(C) I need to go to get some directions.

Answer **(a)**

12. **When can we talk about the crucial issue of dismissal?**

(A) No, discussion is not required tomorrow.

(B) Just after the board meeting

(C) I would like to talk about it.

Answer (b)

13. **When do you open the grocery shop?**

(A) It's close to my grocery store.

(B) At a different shop

(C) Every day at 9:00 a.m.

Answer (c)

14. **Do you want me to bring the finished report today or tomorrow?**

(A) Anytime you are free.

(B) Not in my life time

(C) He finished it very early.

Answer (a)

15. **How can we satisfy the new customers?**

(A) I'll put satisfy him.

(B) Quality is the best strategy.

(C) New comers were late.

Answer (b)

16. **Do you mind opening the window for the fresh air?**

(A) No, go ahead. It's very stuffy in here.
(B) Thank you for changing windows.
(C) The orange is not fresh in the room.

Answer **(a)**

17. **Who is the designer of the new building?**

(A) OK, we'll design it soon.
(B) An architecture in our development department
(C) Just sign to get the building.

Answer **(b)**

18. **Would you like to visit me tomorrow? I am busy right now.**

(A) No, our office is closed.
(B) I'd love to. I will come here again.
(C) What do you mean by that?

Answer **(b)**

19. **How often do you meet your boss?**

(A) Once in a day I see him to report the sales figures.
(B) It's in the meeting room.
(C) I haven't had a meal yet.

Answer **(a)**

20. **Has the research scientist's flight been delayed?**

(A) Has he signed off on it?
(B) I can look up this status on my phone.
(C) He specializes in ancient Greek languages.

Answer (a)

21. **Who's in charge of building the new tower?**

(A) Until August 30th.
(B) Mike is not leaving today.
(C) My senior manager

Answer (c)

22. **Are you interested in the new opening in my company?**

(A) Sure, how do I send the email to your company?
(B) They are not interested in it.
(C) We already opened it.

Answer (a)

23. **Our newly launched project is going well, isn't it?**

(A) Definitely yes.
(B) Every project is not easy.
(C) It was a new event.

Answer (a)

24. **Are you satisfying with your pay?**

(A) No, I want it to be increased.

(B) The payroll is dealt with Mrs. Kempton.

(C) After I pay for it.

Answer (a)

25. **Does the front desk know you are a new comer?**

(A) A new comer should be careful all the time.

(B) The front des is always busy.

(C) No, I told them several times, but they don't recognize me.

Answer (c)

26. **Can I get the new brochures for the concert?**

(A) Sure, I'll go to the concert.

(B) It's a new brochure.

(C) Yes, just pick them up at the front desk.

Answer (c)

27. **Do you know what time the meeting will be finished?**

(A) At around 9 p.m.

(B) Yes, I have met him.

(C) The team will finish the project soon.

Answer (a)

28. **Excuse me, Doctor, when do you want me to see you again?**

(A) See you again when I am free

(B) At the hall

(C) Just when you have your sore back again.

Answer (c)

29. **Who is the best person for the position?**

(A) The position is not opened yet.

(B) Mr. Jason Geeambee

(C) Thanks, I can take care of it.

Answer (b)

30. **Does your boss want you to leave your company now?**

(A) It's very convenient.

(B) I'm not sure. but he is mad at my poor performance.

(C) I will stay for the night.

Answer (b)

Chapter 5. Wedding

Paragraph Challenge 5

Questions 1-4 refer to the following paragraph.

You should be notified that next year we are going to 1.______the tag price of the winter outfits. We are 2.______ pressure from the risen cost in manufacturing winter jackets and trench coats mainly due to the expensive imported clothing materials. The tariffs for the clothing material have been risen up to 10 % 3. ______ to those of last year. Hopefully you will understand the hardship of our company is facing now. You can contact our sales department anytime to consult the quality and 4.______ of our winter outfits. Thank you.

01. (A) increase
(B) riser
(C) rising
(D) increasing

Answer (a)

02. (A) get
(B) getting
(C) gotten
(D) gets

Answer (b)

03. (A) compared
(B) comes
(C) comparison
(D) coming

Answer (a)

04. (A) much
(B) quantity
(C) many
(D) block

Answer (b)

Conversation Challenge 5

01. **Why don't we leave a week earlier so we can buy a cheeper ticket?**

(A) Yes, they were earlier than we expected.
(B) I'm leaving by the theater.
(C) Good idea. I'll check the prices tomorrow.

Answer **(c)**

02. **Have the mechanics finished fixing the plant equipment?**

(A) Yes, they had their job done, sir.
(B) I don't think she's finished.
(C) I haven't decided when to plant them.

Answer **(a)**

03. **Who's going to replace the broken copier?**

(A) I called the mechanic who can take care of it.
(B) Yes, he was paying with it.
(C) The window was broken.

Answer **(a)**

04. **You found an apartment to rent, didn't you?**

(A) Yes, in the down town yesterday

(B) Unfortunately , I'm still using it.

(C) Yes, I lent it to my customer.

Answer **(a)**

05. **Would you like to join the annual party for the company?**

(A) No, I don't like to go to the doctor's.

(B) Sure, I go to the party all the time.

(C) Actually, I was not in there.

Answer **(b)**

06. **What did you say to Allan Karlson?**

(A) I just asked him whether he was good or not.

(B) No, he didn't know what he said.

(C) At the front desk.

Answer **(a)**

07. **How are you going to get the Grand Central Park from here?**

(A) I should be there by 9:30.

(B) I'll take a taxi to get there.

(C) Yes, I'll start to work next day.

Answer **(b)**

08. **Aren't you moving tomorrow, Mr. Parkerson?**

(A) No, I bought the tables last week.
(B) Yes, but I need the extra money.
(C) No, not until I can find out another place.

Answer (c)

09. **Where's the office of the chairman in this building?**

(A) At the 11th floor
(B) The head master will bring you a menu, sir.
(C) There's nobody in this building.

Answer (a)

10. **Why were you late for the luncheon today?**

(A) Because he couldn't change the form.
(B) No, he wasn't able to make the change.
(C) I am sorry, due to the traffic jam.

Answer (c)

11. **Would you like to have your dessert right now, sir?**

(A) I think I've seen enough for the day.
(B) No, not right now after enjoying the main plate.
(C) I think I can wait to taste the dessert tomorrow.

Answer (b)

12. **When do you think the notebook will be mended?**

(A) The man will keep your notebook.

(B) They'll have it mended.

(C) When the mechanic finishes his job for it.

Answer (c)

13. **Do you want to take a break right now or later?**

(A) I have some problems with the brakes.

(B) I'm sorry, I didn't mean to break it.

(C) I am really tired. Let's have it at the moment.

Answer (c)

14. **How about playing tennis this weekend, Barbie?**

(A) No, I played there last week.

(B) My wife and I are going out tonight.

(C) It sounds perfect.

Answer (c)

15. **How about retiring from your company?**

(A) I haven't heard anything yet.

(B) No, it's not an emergency.

(C) No way, I can work for the company until I am 80.

Answer (c)

16. **Do you remember that we are going to have a date tomorrow?**

(A) Sorry, but I already had a date.
(B) Absolutely, I am expecting it.
(C) What are you doing right now?

Answer **(b)**

17. **Can I take a look at your sales report, Mrs. Camelia?**

(A) In a minute, it will be put your desk, sir.
(B) The sales doesn't go well.
(C) Sure, you can examine the sales team.

Answer **(a)**

18. **Where do you want to go for your summer leave?**

(A) The summer leave is very short.
(B) I am going nowhere. Let me catch some sleep.
(C) We spent a week for the summer leave.

Answer **(b)**

19. **Could you get me a few copies for this page?**

(A) Sure, I'll do it right now.
(B) No, I didn't get copies.
(C) I don't think I can fix the copier.

Answer **(a)**

20. **How much is installing the solar panels?**

(A) The ones I bought last year were broken

(B) Yes, the panel is ready to talk about it.

(C) It depends on how large those are.

Answer (c)

21. **Who is going to handle the problems of budgeting?**

(A) Yes, the law firm of Parkersons will take care of it.

(B) No decision has been mJanet yet.

(C) The department of planning and budget

Answer (c)

22. **Are you planning to travel Italy this week?**

(A) Yes, how did you know that?

(B) The last two weeks for Italy.

(C) It's such a beautiful time for sightseeing.

Answer (a)

23. **Do you think that we should have the written statement?**

(A) I also think he is right.

(B) That may be wrong to think about it.

(C) Yes, just for the case of any problems

Answer (c)

24. **Do you know the reason of cancelling the seminar.**

(A) Something came up due to the severe weather
(B) No, I can cancel it.
(C) I know we should attend the seminar.

Answer **(a)**

25. **Is smoking allowed in here? Mr. Dennison?**

(A) Yes, it is the point for you.
(B) No, I stayed in the room and did not smoke there.
(C) Yes, the allowance is not enough.

Answer **(a)**

26. **What are you going to do for your living?**

(A) We are not living until 100.
(B) Yes, living isn't easy.
(C) Don't worry. I have an enough pension.

Answer **(c)**

27. **I heard your company was suffering from the huge deficit.**

(A) No, we don't have any money.
(B) Yes, but we already got over it.
(C) Yes, we have a big company.

Answer **(b)**

28. **Did you have any locker in this building?**

(A) Yes, but you should get the permission from the maintenance department for the use of it.

(B) Not in my yard

(C) Right after they locked the door.

Answer (a)

29. **When do you want to have your test? now or tomorrow?**

(A) Yes, I think you are right.

(B) I would do it right now.

(C) Tomorrow is much better for me.

Answer (c)

30. **Why don't we have steak at the fancy diner in the down town?**

(A) I am sorry, I am out of the budget this week.

(B) You have a good dine.

(C) Yes, we are late for the diner.

Answer (a)

Chapter 6. Bakery

Paragraph Challenge 6

Questions 1-4 refer to the following paragraph.

Beginning on Nov. 1st, we will be using a new banking service that will 1.______ your bank account. First, your online and mobile banking will be 2.______ temporarily from Oct.30 to Oct. 31st. Be careful when you use your electronic banking on those days. Second, You should 3.________ the newly reinforced security program for your secured banking. Thank you in advance 4______ your cooperation and understanding.

01. (A) affecting
(B) affectionate
(C) affect
(D) affection

Answer (c)

02. (A) closed
(B) correct
(C) reject
(D) entered

Answer (a)

03. (A) down
(B) download
(C) disturb
(D) distributing

Answer (b)

04. (A) for
(B) after
(C) before
(D) between

Answer (a)

Conversation Challenge 6

01. **Where are you going to take Mr. Johnson out to lunch?**

(A) At 3:30

(B) No, he has another appointment.

(C) To a fancy restaurant.

Answer **(c)**

02. **Are you going to leave for New York?**

(A) No, it's too expensive.

(B) Yes, it is my fist time to go there.

(C) I should make it on time.

Answer **(b)**

03. **I am sorry to interrupt you but would you like me to help you?**

(A) Yes, it is busy.

(B) No, I didn't give him my thought

(C) No, thank you. That's all right.

Answer **(c)**

04. **That milk in the refrigerator doesn't look very fresh, does it?**

(A) I would agree.

(B) He doesn't it meat.

(C) Yes, it does.

Answer (c)

05. **What will you do this afternoon, Mrs Kate?**

(A) They want to postpone the meeting until tomorrow.

(B) Well, I have no plans right now.

(C) They will do it on that side.

Answer (b)

06. **How many board members are coming to the meeting?**

(A) Yes, many people are shopping there.

(B) Only 5 of them

(C) I bought them through my stockbroker.

Answer (b)

07. **Is the copy machine working well now?**

(A) Because I am cone using it.

(B) No, it should be taken care of by a mechanic.

(C) No, he wasn't able to get it done.

Answer (b)

08. **How much is the rate of this package, Mrs. Hellen?**

(A) No, I put them on the floor.
(B) Mary set then on her desk.
(C) Sorry, I don't know it yet.

Answer **(c)**

09. **Why don't we have a fresh air and break?**

(A) Because the car was going to fast.
(B) Yeah, I need some fresh air.
(C) Yes, it is a good idea.

Answer **(c)**

10. **What are you going to do in the near future?**

(A) I want to have my own business in two years.
(B) I have to fly over to Disney Land.
(C) Yes, that plan does look good.

Answer **(a)**

11. **How can I get to the new airport in New York?**

(A) Yes, you should be able to.
(B) You'd better take a taxi.
(C) No, I want to stay in New York.

Answer **(b)**

12. **Did you get your car fixed yesterday?**

(A) I put it under my car.
(B) No, I could not make an arrangement for it.
(C) Yes, they did not fix it.

Answer (b)

13. **How are you doing these days, Mr. Parkerson?**

(A) I am quite good, thank you.
(B) No, I'll go the day after tomorrow.
(C) Terribly sorry about that.

Answer (a)

14. **When is your doctor's appointment, Mr. Kensington?**

(A) At that new clinic downstairs.
(B) No, it isn't.
(C) At 2:30 today

Answer (c)

15. **You haven't sent out my parcel yet, have you?**

(A) Don't worry. It is delivered by the courier service.
(B) Yes, it does smell nice, doesn't it?
(C) No, I don't have to.

Answer (a)

16. **Who will take over your job when you leave your company?**

(A) It is not decided yet.

(B) It hasn't been late.

(C) Mark Brown is moving now.

Answer (a)

17. **Do you need the report to be done tomorrow, boss?**

(A) Who know?

(B) We need not your boss.

(C) I'd like it today if it is possible.

Answer (c)

18. **Could you tell me the way to the forest in the Central Park?**

(A) Absolutely, go strait from the intersection.

(B) I wasn't able to go the park.

(C) Yes, I already put in the park.

Answer (a)

19. **How much longer do I have to wait in line for the concert?**

(A) I only have to go for two blocs for the concert.

(B) In about 20 minutes

(C) He wants me to reduce the line.

Answer (b)

20. **What are you going to do when you have your leave?**

(A) That the leave isn't long enough.
(B) I haven't decided yet.
(C) No, I don't think it right.

Answer (b)

21. **Where can I get my notebook fixed?**

(A) Yes, you can fix it.
(B) At the after sales service center
(C) She doesn't like notebooks.

Answer (b)

22. **How do you like your new company, Johnson?**

(A) Oh, it's the best apartment.
(B) I wish I still had my former job.
(C) I have a great time.

Answer (b)

23. **What time do you want me to pick you up at the airport, Karl?**

(A) Yes, I think I have time.
(B) Around 7:00 PM
(C) Yes, could you please?

Answer (c)

24. **How about your marketing job, Mr. Delkerson?**

(A) Until now, it is good.
(B) It's usually done for marketing.
(C) Yes, he was a marketer.

Answer (a)

25. **How come you have spent so much money last month?**

(A) Yes, that was much money.
(B) I had a big loss in the stock market.
(C) She had spent money.

Answer (b)

26. **When do you think I should take a picture?**

(A) Right after the show
(B) I think you should not draw a picture.
(C) Let me decide to take a picture.

Answer (a)

27. **Are you tired, Mrs. Dolton? You look so shabby.**

(A) Yes, they were all tired.
(B) Yes, I could not catch a sleep last night.
(C) No, I still feel tired.

Answer (b)

28. **That dinner was really fantastic in honor of Mrs. Peterson.**

(A) Yes, I enjoyed it very much.

(B) No, it's wrong to talk about her honor.

(C) Yes, she was quite good.

Answer (a)

29. **Can you speak other languages except English?**

(A) I can't. I just command only English.

(B) Yes, they speak English.

(C) Only a little bit.

Answer (a)

30. **Fill out this form for your medical checkup.**

(A) Yes, I will do it right now.

(B) How much is it?

(C) Sorry, we don't have anymore checkup for you.

Answer (a)

Chapter 7. 7Technology

Paragraph Challenge 7

Questions 1–4 refer to the following paragraph.

You are receiving the e–mail concerning the 1.________ of a password change for your T band for MK Teleservice. Your 2.______ has been settled again, and you should change your password. Please be notified that it will 3.______ at least one hour or so for the total change. Log on to www. mkteleservice. com. Please complete the form, and change your password according to the 4.________ given on the page. Thank you all the time for your loyalty and long–term use of our service.

01. (A) request
(B) requested
(C) requesting
(D) requests

Answer **(a)**

02. (A) account
(B) accountant
(C) accounts
(D) accountable

Answer (a)

03. (A) taken
(B) taking
(C) took
(D) take

Answer (d)

04. (A) induction
(B) introduction
(C) intake
(D) instructions

Answer (d)

Conversation Challenge 7

01. **What is the special menu at this diner?**

(A) Yes, I've had enough dinner.
(B) Good idea.
(C) Meat pasta with cheese, sir

Answer (c)

02. **How long do I have to wait for your new book?**

(A) It was am hour ago.
(B) It will take at least two more days
(C) I think you books are interesting.

Answer (b)

03. **Do you know where the restroom is in this precinct?**

(A) The rest rooms are full of people.
(B) There is one outside this building.
(C) You can rest in that chair.

Answer (b)

04. **Can you notify me when you can complete this project?**

(A) No, I haven't finished it yet.

(B) I started on it yesterday.

(C) By the end of the week.

Answer (c)

05. **Do you want to grab a bite to eat with me, Jackson?**

(A) Don't pull so hard.

(B) That sounds perfect!

(C) I think it's fish and chips.

Answer (b)

06. **How many pages for the new website are you preparing?**

(A) I plan to page it now.

(B) More than 20

(C) I thought it was pretty prepared.

Answer (b)

07. **How do you come to your office, do you drive yourself?**

(A) Yes, I will get my driver's license next month.

(B) Actually, I commute by subway

(C) The bus is not probably faster than the metro.

Answer (b)

08. **How did you find out the new client for the company?**

(A) It depends on where you want to see the client.

(B) It is the result of my trial to contact latent customers.

(C) We'll need the company.

Answer **(b)**

09. **When is the anniversary of your company?**

(A) Today is the day.

(B) It's downtown Norton Road 13th.

(C) Next month, he will celebrate his birthday.

Answer **(a)**

10. **What do you want for your dish of lunch?**

(A) Oil Pane pasta

(B) We wash the dish all the time.

(C) They said it was not lunch time.

Answer **(a)**

11. **Would you tell me how shipping fees are charged, Mr. Markerson?**

(A) How much are they?

(B) It depends on the weight as far as I know.

(C) Wrap this item separately, please.

Answer **(b)**

12. **David, do we have any problems with the network connectivity?**

(A) Yes, I'm living alone.

(B) The online is closed today.

(C) I am leaving at 6:00.

Answer **(b)**

13. **How do you calculate population in the region near San Francisco?**

(A) By the measurement provided by Indexon company

(B) It's a casual affair.

(C) No, I am not going to the fair.

Answer **(b)**

14. **Would you mind using your mobile phone for a moment?**

(A) No, I haven't used it.

(B) I'm sorry, it is now out of electricity.

(C) Don't mind about the use.

Answer **(b)**

15. **How do you contact your boss when he is out of town?**

(A) The boss calls me when he needs.

(B) The boss's looking forward to her trip to New York.

(C) I think the boss was busy.

Answer **(a)**

16. **What is your preference on the choice of your jacket?**

(A) It's my favorite color.
(B) The late comer is not chooser.
(C) I like red color of it.

Answer (c)

17. **Where do you want to go for dinner, Meggy?**

(A) I want to go to Mandarine Diner
(B) I'm going to dine now.
(C) The dinner is expensive, Meg

Answer (a)

18. **What are you going to take metro or a taxi?**

(A) I love training every day.
(B) My preference is my car.
(C) Yes, I walked to the station.

Answer (b)

19. **Have you met our new client, Mrs. Melanie?**

(A) Yes, we had a meeting already.
(B) Yes, I live with a client.
(C) No, I am not meeting you anymore.

Answer (a)

20. **Who was in charge of completing the new project?**

(A) Mr. Jackson is the head of it.
(B) They completed their mission.
(C) The charge is ten dollars.

Answer (a)

21. **When do you expect they can give a hand on the project?**

(A) I actually thought it was handy.
(B) By the end of this week, maybe.
(C) I think we can give him a thought.

Answer (b)

22. **Are you supposed to meet our managing director, Malcom?**

(A) I've never met Malcom.
(B) No, I don't know him.
(C) Actually, the meeting was cancelled.

Answer (c)

23. **They could not get in touch with the new comers, do you know the reason?**

(A) I was recruited upon graduation.
(B) And how was the result?
(C) They moved to another company before coming to us.

Answer (c)

24. **Where do you want to go for your winter vacation, Pamela?**

(A) I love to go to Switzerland for skiing.
(B) My vacation is quite long.
(C) It's too cold in winter.

Answer (a)

25. **Are you happy with your transfer to the new department?**

(A) Absolutely, I am so happy.
(B) Yes, I can transfer to the new one.
(C) I am not moving to other company.

Answer (a)

26. **Why don't we take a ten minute break before the next performance?**

(A) Yes, I've love to take it.
(B) I can say it is possible for the braking system.
(C) I think we can break it.

Answer (a)

27. **Do you have a reservation for the Nelson Hotel?**

(A) I am still thinking about going.
(B) Yes, on Dec. 12th, confirmed.
(C) The place must be busy.

Answer (b)

28. **When do you think you can you fill out this survey?**

(A) I'd be glad to.

(B) I'll file them this afternoon.

(C) It will take in about 10 minutes.

Answer (c)

29. **Can you go out with me for the new movie?**

(A) Sure, why don't we meet at 7:00?

(B) It was more entertaining than the first movie.

(C) My father saw the movie.

Answer (a)

30. **The new gadgetry will cost me an arm and a leg.**

(A) I'll send you my cost.

(B) I know, it is too expensive.

(C) The final cost is not fixed yet.

Answer (b)

Chapter 8. Reading

Paragraph Challenge 8

Questions 1–4 refer to the following paragraph.

As you know, the number of population in L.A. has risen 1.________ over 5 years. Due to the increased number of 2.________ in the city, we have faced the problems of costly living cost and inflation of prices surrounding communities. Also the cost of available local housing is 3.______ the rise. Insufficient living condition results in more increased matters of the homeless. It 4.________ to me that the municipal authorities will take care of those problems for the well being of the citizens.

01. (A) climb
(B) significantly
(C) significant
(D) climbing

Answer (b)

02. (A) residing
(B) reside
(C) residential
(D) residents

Answer (d)

03. (A) to
(B) beyond
(C) to
(D) on

Answer (d)

04. (A) occurred
(B) expended
(C) approached
(D) experimented

Answer (a)

Conversation Challenge 8

01. **Who told you about your company's M&A?**

(A) I told him that he is in charge of it.

(B) You're a M&A merchant.

(C) It was announced in yesterday's boarding meeting.

Answer (c)

02. **How far is Dalevill from here, Mr. Molton?**

(A) I don't know, but it is quite a long distance.

(B) John lives in Dalevill.

(C) We're going there tomorrow.

Answer (a)

03. **Why don't you tell Mr. Johnson for your pay raise?**

(A) I'm afraid he will refuse it.

(B) Of course I'll help my friend.

(C) No, they didn't tell me the truth.

Answer (a)

04. **Can you tell me the exact way to Maxim street?**

(A) It is 100 percent increase from my offer.
(B) You should take the route No. 2 from here.
(C) You should have your own Maxim.

Answer (b)

05. **How much is the cost to have our old house remodeled?**

(A) The estimate is 10,000 dollars.
(B) By next day, they will set to remodel the house.
(C) The living room is remodeled.

Answer (a)

06. **Can you tell me when the courier service will come?**

(A) I'll let you know what is it.
(B) I think the service will not come to us, today.
(C) You delivered a package for us.

Answer (b)

07. **I don't know where is the rest room for men.**

(A) She's in the rest room.
(B) I'm new here, too. Please ask a janitor over there.
(C) I am not going to the rest room.

Answer (b)

08. **Can you tell me where the office of chairman?**

(A) This is the chairman.

(B) The chairman's name is John Walker.

(C) It's on the top floor of the building.

Answer (c)

09. **How much do you want to have your hair cut?**

(A) I'd like to use a shortcut.

(B) As short as it is.

(C) I go to a salon every day.

Answer (b)

10. **Do you like to watch SF movies, Janet?**

(A) Yes, they taste sweet.

(B) No, I am a big fan of San Francisco.

(C) That's my favorite type of movies.

Answer (c)

11. **When does the boss want the report to be done?**

(A) I thought the boss went out with it.

(B) It is due next week.

(C) Leave it on the boss' desk.

Answer (b)

12. **Do you subscribe a Messenger Daily online?**

(A) Yes, every day by my mobile phone.
(B) Every weekend is good for me.
(C) Yes, she does.

Answer (a)

13. **Why do you buy the apartment? You are leaving here.**

(A) No, I like to buy it now.
(B) For the investment
(C) I haven't decided it yet.

Answer (b)

14. **Weren't you supposed to walk your dog every day?**

(A) I think it's okay to walk the dog.
(B) I got up late with the news.
(C) I couldn't. I was sick today.

Answer (c)

15. **Who will be the mechanic to take care of the oil change for the car?**

(A) I think Mr. Conrad is a professional.
(B) I chose Mr. Parkerson for it.
(C) Taking care of it is hard for me.

Answer (b)

16. **Do you stress the importance of being on time to your employees?**

(A) Yes, It is very important.

(B) At 9 A.M., I guess.

(C) No, I don't think it is well done.

Answer (a)

17. **How can we get to the place of Mr. Dickerson's birthday party?**

(A) We can take a bus from the exit 9 from the gate of the metro station.

(B) It's not too far.

(C) I want to see him someday.

Answer (a)

18. **Shall I take you more papers and ink from the storage room?**

(A) This printer is out of ink.

(B) The extra paper is in the storage room.

(C) Yes, you should. Thank you for your help.

Answer (c)

19. **How are you presenting your newly released car today?**

(A) It is going well and I am happy.

(B) I want it presented in the show.

(C) I'd like to, but I can't release it.

Answer (a)

20. **Would you mind recommending Mr. Johnson as CEO of our company?**

(A) It's too late.

(B) No, he is the perfect for the position.

(C) That's quite expensive, as far as I know.

Answer (b)

21. **Can you tell me when the speaker will come for the seminar?**

(A) She will be here in half an hour.

(B) No, I don't think he really speaks.

(C) Actually, he seemed to speak well.

Answer (a)

22. **Don't you have your insurance renewed?**

(A) Yes, I mailed the insurance for you.

(B) I've already have it extended.

(C) Yes, I'm happy with the insurance.

Answer (b)

23. **Do you remember to make a reservation for the air line?**

(A) Of course. It has already been confirmed on December 24th.

(B) There are too many air lines.

(C) Yes, everyone got a reservation.

Answer (a)

24. **I heard Mr. Parkerson got promoted last month.**

(A) Since he was born

(B) Congratulations!

(C) Who told you?

Answer (c)

25. **Is the new employee in the department of accounting?**

(A) That's right, he is a novice now.

(B) He just walks in the morning.

(C) Yes, the department is dealing with the accounting.

Answer (a)

26. **What are the requirements to apply for the company?**

(A) Gilbert is a very hard worker.

(B) At least five year's experience in the accounting

(C) You could probably work for the day shift.

Answer (b)

27. **Who will participate in the negotiation with the Chinese company?**

(A) In the large meeting room.

(B) They negotiated the whole morning.

(C) Mr. Karltopher will do it.

Answer (c)

28. **Would you like to go to the movies tonight with me?**

(A) I have to go with you, since I love to.

(B) I am a little bit late.

(C) It comes to 100 dollars.

Answer (a)

29. **Do you know why Mrs. Susie is late tonight?**

(A) Well, I hear so.

(B) Yes, she does.

(C) She's called in sick ten minutes ago.

Answer (c)

30. **Are you going to sign up for the class next semester?**

(A) Be careful, the sign board can fall anytime.

(B) Yes, I am. I heard the professor is the top authorities in the chemistry.

(C) We have the autographs of the celebrities.

Answer (b)

Chapter 9. Food

Paragraph Challenge 9

Questions 1–4 refer to the following paragraph.

For the coffee lovers a doctor says that you have no problems when you drink as 1.______ as you want. The doctor is professor, Durex, who is one of the authorities on coffee, a director of the Institute for Coffee Studies at New York University. He's even 2.________ a metric for monitoring your dosage. But the doctor recommends that you should 3.______ back on the consumption of coffee only when you can't sleep at night. If you don't have any problems with your sleep at night, he advises that you can drink to the amount you like. He also insists that it's not going to do you any 4.______, and it will actually help you.

01. (A) much
(B) lighter
(C) many
(D) lot

Answer **(a)**

02. (A) added
(B) imitated
(C) developed
(D) said

Answer (c)

03. (A) drink
(B) increase
(C) cut
(D) drop

Answer (c)

04. (A) harmed
(B) harms
(C) harm
(D) harmful

Answer (c)

Conversation Challenge 9

01. **Where Mr. Parkerson is going for his business trip?**

(A) I have a meeting at 12:00.
(B) You want to go to lunch with them?
(C) He is planning to leave for L.A.

Answer **(c)**

02. **When do you want my report to be submitted?**

(A) About 10 reports
(B) It should be reported.
(C) No later than next Tuesday

Answer **(c)**

03. **Why did they postpone the board meeting?**

(A) Yes, I met them.
(B) Because something urgent happened.
(C) It was a real surprise.

Answer **(b)**

04. **What was your job when you worked for Tompson Inc.?**

(A) I went to Tompson last month.

(B) I worked as an accountant.

(C) Business is not easy at all.

Answer (b)

05. **Have you ever accomplished your dream of being a lawyer?**

(A) No, I can't even imagine it.

(B) Absolutely, I already became a partner at the law firm.

(C) The whole dreamer was too foolish.

Answer (b)

06. **How do you make this sofa so comfortable?**

(A) We use the expensive and effective latex for it.

(B) No thank you. I've had made it.

(C) I guess it's not easy.

Answer (a)

07. **Do we have to buy the new printer today or tomorrow?**

(A) We don't have to, it has already arrived.

(B) The order is not canceled.

(C) For the news printing system

Answer (a)

08. **How much will it cost to have a new refrigerator?**

(A) By December 11th

(B) I had it checked already.

(C) About over two million dollars

Answer (c)

09. **When did the mechanic say he would come to the office?**

(A) It's under 100 kilometers.

(B) At around 4:00

(C) If you come to the office, we will appreciate it.

Answer (b)

10. **When did you get this project done?**

(A) When you ordered me to do it.

(B) Lots of projects are left.

(C) Let's go over the profect.

Answer (a)

11. **Do you want the department of human resources to hire more?**

(A) Whenever it is possible, we need more people.

(B) And how many people are in there?

(C) Neither do I.

Answer (a)

12. **Who is in charge of taking care of the accounting figures?**

(A) Tompson took the report to look into the figures.

(B) I have an exact figure

(C) Our new comer at the department of budgeting

Answer (c)

13. **Did you have a file for the backup?**

(A) Yes, just for the future use

(B) My back is killing me.

(C) We go back to check the file.

Answer (a)

14. **Will you forward your e-mail to the boss, today?**

(A) Nobody e-mail me.

(B) Don't worry. I already did the job.

(C) Thank you so much.

Answer (b)

15. **What happened to the banks today?**

(A) They are all closed because of holidays.

(B) Yes, it's the new holiday.

(C) No, problem.

Answer (a)

16. **Would you like to work as a full-timer for the company?**

(A) That makes sense.
(B) Absolutely, I want to.
(C) That's not important for the boss.

Answer (b)

17. **What is the address of our supplier for the main boards?**

(A) It's 522 at Kensington Street.
(B) The supplier is not here.
(C) I think it's the important board.

Answer (a)

18. **How about mending your presentation script before it starts.**

(A) No, I don't know the presentation.
(B) Actually, I already did.
(C) Mind your manner.

Answer (b)

19. **Do you have any pills for a toothache?**

(A) I have my tooth pulled out.
(B) Yes, I have a painkiller now.
(C) That's the worst.

Answer (b)

20. **How about accepting the new offer?**

(A) I didn't say a word.

(B) We offer a 50 percent discount.

(C) Well, I will just stay at this company.

Answer (c)

21. **How often do I have to check the e-mails for the company?**

(A) I wash my car checked yet.

(B) Twice a day before you leave the office.

(C) I'll e-mail you right now.

Answer (b)

22. **Do you like to use your smart watch?**

(A) Here's my watch.

(B) No, it is not short.

(C) Yes, it is very convenient.

Answer (c)

23. **I heard you earned enormous amount of money.**

(A) Yes, I was so lucky.

(B) I put it back in my wallet.

(C) They made a lot of efforts.

Answer (a)

24. **When do you want to go on a picnic for us?**

(A) We are going to go on a picnic to the beach.
(B) Anytime will be fine.
(C) Probably we are moving the furniture.

Answer (b)

25. **Are you going to go to celebrate the boss's birthday?**

(A) Yes, I am inviting the boss.
(B) No, I am leaving for New York.
(C) I like the boss.

Answer (b)

26. **Will you join us for playing chess, Dave?**

(A) Why are you late?
(B) Yes, it is my favorite.
(C) I am late, too.

Answer (b)

27. **Do you think I should send this parcel before the Christmas Day?**

(A) Sure, you are in charge of it.
(B) There's a mailbox for him.
(C) I bought a Christmas parcel yesterday.

Answer (a)

28. **Could you tell me about the cause of your success?**

(A) Yes, I could tell you that I worked almost 16 hours a day.

(B) Sure, what do you want to hear?

(C) Today is a very successful day.

Answer (a)

29. **How did you make the sales figures?**

(A) I figured them out now.

(B) Sales dramatically plummeted last month.

(C) It was based on the data you gave to me.

Answer (c)

30. **I'm planning to buy you a new smart phone.**

(A) Yes, the new smart phone is good.

(B) You are not smart guy.

(C) Wow, I am really happy with the news.

Answer (c)

Chapter 10. Dining

Paragraph Challenge 10

Questions 1-4 refer to the following paragraph.

Your intent of taking a vacation is a good 1._______. Travelling for recreation is sometimes a luxury that only wealthy people can 2._______. But nowadays, many people in the world are enjoying travelling by means of 3.________ a vacation. Regardless of their income and wealth, people are happy when they are taking a break from work. But, as you know, it is 4._________ that you should take the permission from your supervisor before your leave when you are employed.

01. (A) idea
(B) day
(C) ideas
(D) days

Answer (a)

02. (A) affording
(B) affords
(C) affordable
(D) afford

Answer (d)

03. (A) takes
(B) taking
(C) taken
(D) take

Answer (b)

04. (A) wish
(B) required
(C) requires
(D) wishes

Answer (b)

Conversation Challenge 10

01. **Mrs. Callaway, where do you want to go with Mr. Markerson for lunch?**

(A) At 10:00

(B) No, he is not here.

(C) To an Indian diner

Answer (c)

02. **When are you going to leave for L.A.?**

(A) No, it's too late.

(B) In two days

(C) I should go to L.A.

Answer (b)

03. **If you are not busy, would you show me how to use the copier?**

(A) Yes, here is the copier.

(B) No, I don't want you to use it.

(C) Sure, wait a moment

Answer (c)

04. **The milk in the refrigerator doesn't look good to drink.**

(A) It's gone, be careful not to have it.
(B) He doesn't eat milk.
(C) No, I didn't drink milk.

Answer (a)

05. **What's the agenda for today's board meeting?**

(A) You should know that it has been canceled.
(B) Yes, the agenda is important.
(C) They will board the train.

Answer (a)

06. **How many applicants apply for the company?**

(A) More than 200.
(B) As much as I can.
(C) I applied for it yesterday.

Answer (a)

07. **Do we have to fix the camera, today?**

(A) Because I am not taking the photos.
(B) No, it is not that urgent.
(C) Yes, the camera is expensive.

Answer (b)

08. **Who will pick up the package in the lobby?**

(A) No, the package is expensive to be delivered.
(B) Let me take care of it, while I am going there.
(C) The lobby is always busy.

Answer (b)

09. **What do you want for your birthday present?**

(A) Because the present boss is a smart leader.
(B) A piece of new glasses
(C) Yes, it is my birthday.

Answer (b)

10. **What are you planning to do for your summer leave?**

(A) I will travel Italy this time.
(B) I have to fly over to L.A.
(C) Yes, planning is important.

Answer (a)

11. **How can I get to the Melvil Hotel?**

(A) Yes, you should be able to.
(B) You'd better take the bus No. 110 at the bus stop.
(C) No, I want to walk alone.

Answer (b)

12. **What do you do for your living?**

(A) I put it in the living room.

(B) No, they will live up to 100.

(C) I am a sales man.

Answer (c)

13. **How are you doing these days, Mrs. Pamela?**

(A) I am quite good.

(B) No, I'll do it right now.

(C) I am so young to go to school.

Answer (a)

14. **When are you going to see your professor?**

(A) At the living room

(B) No, the professor is not here.

(C) He wants to have a meeting with me at 10:00.

Answer (c)

15. **Who is your boss to make the final decision on the project?**

(A) The man sitting on the chair in the office.

(B) Yes, it it final.

(C) No, I don't like the project.

Answer (a)

16. **Is Mr. Johnson your successor, Amelia?**

(A) Yes, he's a nice guy.
(B) He is in charge of our company.
(C) I think so.

Answer (c)

17. **When are you going to have the presentation?**

(A) Yes, I have to present it.
(B) We need our presentation.
(C) Maybe next Friday

Answer (c)

18. **How long will it take to get to the airport from here?**

(A) More than an hour
(B) I wasn't ready to go to the airport.
(C) The airport is very huge.

Answer (a)

19. **When is your apartment's house warming party?**

(A) Next Monday evening
(B) The apartment is not large enough.
(C) He wants me to go to the apartment.

Answer (a)

20. **Who is in charge of dealing with the contract?**

(A) I should be in charge of the bill.
(B) My boss is handling it.
(C) No, I don't know the contract.

Answer (b)

21. **The refrigerator is out of order now, what should I do?**

(A) Yes, the fridge is the ordered one.
(B) I like to buy the refrigerator.
(C) Just call the department of customer service to take care of it.

Answer (c)

22. **Is Johnson & Johnson Inc. located near here?**

(A) Yes, it is just next to our building
(B) I will locate the lost item.
(C) We are not satisfied with it.

Answer (a)

23. **How about the sales figure of this month?**

(A) It is quite good, but the boss is not satisfied with it.
(B) We can figure it out.
(C) We have no sales team.

Answer (a)

24. **How do you get to your workplace?**

(A) The place is closed today.
(b) The workplace is really far away from his home.
(C) I go to work on foot every day.

Answer **(c)**

25. **Is the company a spinoff from the conglomerate?**

(A) Not at all, it is a big company itself.
(B) No, I can take it off.
(C) The company is far away off the main street.

Answer **(a)**

26. **Excuse me, can you tell me the way to operate the new software?**

(A) Mind your own business.
(B) I don't think it is the right software.
(C) Sure thing, I will be right back to you.

Answer **(c)**

27. **Is the insurance covering all the expenses of a car accident?**

(A) Yes, they are covering us.
(B) Definitely, every cost of it.
(C) No, it is his insurance.

Answer **(b)**

28. **Thank you for the wonderful dinner, Mr. Wood.**

(A) You're welcome. I am happy with your content.
(B) No, it's not a dinner but a lunch.
(C) Yes, it is expensive one.

Answer (a)

29. **Do you expect your second baby, Mrs. Kerry?**

(A) Yes, my baby is the top priority.
(B) Yes, he is the second to none.
(C) Yes, I am happy with the truth.

Answer (c)

30. **Why don't you hand the paperwork to the assistant, Marry?**

(A) I should take care of it myself, I think.
(B) There are many assistants.
(C) Yes, you can give me a hand.

Answer (a)

저자 약력

조동인

외국어대학교 영어과 학사 졸업

뉴욕주립대 석사

외국어대학교 문학 박사

현, 인하공업전문대학 어학교양학부 부교수